IT'S ABOUT TIME

Whoopi Goldberg, the Host of The View was correct when she commented that events, disasters, tragedies involving race are not really about race but man's inhumanity to man. We know that race is not a valid term scientifically or historically, so it is an inappropriate term to associate with humanity. What is also associated with humanity is the concept of evolution, the process of development and growth although we think of evolution as being a physical phenomenon, it also applies to our mind and emotions.

In 1st Corinthians 13, of the Bible (KJV), the Apostle Paul spoke about the evolution of minds and emotions when he referred to humanity's growth from childhood to maturity. When we were children we spoke, thought, understood with the mind of a child, but as we matured, we "put away childish things." Over time, things that were not clear to us as children became clear as we evolved into maturity.

American society has lived with the pseudo-science term Race since its beginning and the multitude of conflicts it has invented for humanity. This book provides an opportunity for the reader to remove the degree of the misunderstanding surrounding the concept and its evolution of what serves as the basis of race, namely, the concept of European supremacy.

This book takes a look at the history of ethnic bias beginning in 1137, when Geoffrey of Monmouth in a book of myths entitled, History of the Kings of Britian, identified the Anglo-Saxons as the best people in Britan based on their character and behavior. Although that claim of the best was a myth, the Anglo-Saxons continued to promote it as real. Over several hundred years, the claim of superiority expanded to include the ruling class of males in Europe. The supremacy was not based on skin color or geography until the Europeans began their explorations and subsequent colonization of non-Christian and non-European countries.

This book follows the development of the concept of ethnic bias through popular publications that served to underscore and support the myth of European supremacy. The word race was invented to mean subspecies because the Anglo-Saxons and Europeans made the claim of representing the species of Homo sapiens. Therefore, all non-European people were seen as inferior to them. This book examines the impact that the confusion of race and ethnicity has had on America and how efforts to preserve the myth reveal drastic measures by proponents of the myth.

IT'S ABOUT TIME
LOSING CONTROL OF EUROPEAN SUPREMACY

PAUL R. LEHMAN

CITI OF BOOKS

CITIOFBOOKS, INC.
3736 Eubank NE Suite A1
Albuquerque, NM 87111-3579
www.citiofbooks.com
Hotline: 1 (877) 389-2759
Fax: 1 (505) 930-7244

Ordering Information:
Quantity sales. Special discounts are available on quantity purchases by corporations, associations, and others. For details, contact the publisher at the address above.

Printed in the United States of America.

ISBN-13:	Softcover	979-8-89391-729-1
	eBook	979-8-89391-730-7

Library of Congress Control Number: 2025911426

Table of Contents

DEDICATION

To my Grandchildren

Calvin, Erik, Simone, Robin, Jetta, and Janeel, may the lightof joy, love, happiness, peace, understanding and thankfulnessbrighten your paths always.

ACKNOWLEDGMENT

My sincere appreciation and thanks go out to my family, friends, and associates who supported and encouraged me during this endeavor. Their concern and understanding of my efforts made the experience less difficult and burdensome than it could have been, especially during the pandemic.

A special thank you goes to Mary Lee Dean whose concern, understanding, and encouragement kept me focused on my goal.

FOREWORD

In 1949, Looney Tunes cartoons introduced a character named Wile E. Coyote or Wily Coyote, whose reason for being was to catch Road Runner and satisfy his hunger. Of course, Wile E. Coyote would never achieve his objective because that would end the show. The creators of the cartoon invented him to be the focus and pursuer while the Road Runner defied apprehension. Wile E. Coyote was by no means stupid. He used his knowledge and creativity to devise various plans and equipment to help him achieve his objective. The audience was entertained by the coyote's antics that, on the surface, should work, but due to the Road Runner's ingenuity always fails.

The audience viewed Wile E. Coyote as a sympathetic figure because regardless of what tactics he employed, he would never experience success. If the audience saw the coyote as an entertaining and humorous figure, they gave little thought to the fact that he lacked common sense. Why would the coyote continue to pursue the Road Runner without concluding that he was wasting time and energy in a fruitless effort? If capturing the Road Runner was just to satisfy Wile E. Coyote's hunger, then why didn't he give up the chase and seek other sources of nourishment after so many failed attempts? Again, the story would have only one episode if that were the case.

For over two hundred years segments of American society have been trying to fight, capture, destroy, abolish, and stop racism to no avail. Why? Because, like the Road Runner, racism was invented to withstand any resistance to it. The onus is on Wile E. Coyote to capture the Road Runner, and try as he might, he cannot capture him.

The efforts of the opponents of racism can learn a lesson from this cartoon by asking the question, why does the coyote want to catch the Road Runner? The simple answer is to eat him and satisfy his hunger. If the coyote were to employ his common sense, he might ask himself if the Road Runner is the only food available for him. If not, then the coyote should change his focus and search for food that is more readily available to him. For him to continue to pursue the Road Runner is a waste of time and energy.

Racism is a social concept based on the false premise of race. Race and racism are effects that are visual and experienced in

America based on the myth of European supremacy. Like the Road Runner, race and racism continue to exist because people have come to view them as the cause of ethnic bigotry. While they are not the cause of ethnic bigotry, they have served as distractions from the cause—the myth of European supremacy. If the Coyote continues to focus on catching the Road Runner, he will never satisfy his hunger, and if people continue to seek to destroy race and racism, it will continue to exist. Race is a self- preserving word that grows with each use. No one will argue the devastating history race and racism have caused in America and the world, but to continue focusing on fighting race and racism is not productive. Belief in the myth of European supremacy is what gave birth to the false concept of race, and subsequently, racism. So, the only way to get rid of race and racism is to reveal their truth. To reveal the truth of European supremacy and how it came to control and dominate society, we must look at its history. In the following pages, we hope to enlighten the reader on the history of Anglo-Saxon, European American, and European supremacy.

INTRODUCTION

For over two hundred years the Western world in general and American society in particular, according to history, have accepted the language of race as normal and ordinary. The fact that race is a social invention with no biological basis seems to have had no effect on society. The primary purpose of race is to support, protect, and promote the myth of European supremacy. Once society accepted the language of race, the actual word race did not need to be used in order to achieve the desired results. Society accepted information through the language of race that has been harmful and dangerous by constantly viewing humans as being biologically different from one another.

A recent statement in a *National Geographic* "Biological Differences: Myth Linger," (09/2021 p.16), made reference to "In 2016 a study of around two hundred medical students and residents published by researchers at the University of Virginia found that around half held at least one belief about "biological differences between Blacks and whites, many of which are false and fantastical in nature." The most common myth, according to the statement was "that Black people have a higher tolerance for pain and have thicker skin." What we find in this information relative to biological differences between Black people and whites is a failure to debunk the concept of race in general. Why continue to make references to Black and white people when they do not exist?

A brief article in the AARP Bulletin "Life expectancy plummets in U.S," written by Rachel Ninia in September 2021, is an example of how the language of race works in our everyday lives. The article noted that "The expected longevity for Americans fell by almost 18 months in 2020, the largest drop since World War II, the Centers for Disease Control and Prevention reports." The primary cause of the plunge was COVID-19 which amounted to about three-quarters of the deaths; drugs, according to the article also played a significant role in the drop. The article reported good news for older Americans: "A 60-year-old man can expect to live nearly 23 more years and a 65-year-old woman about 29, almost no change from 2019."

To make clear the effect of the plunge, the article presented a chart to indicate how long Americans are expected to live:

	2019	2020
Overall	78.8 years	77.3 years
Men	76.3 years	74.5 years
Women	81.4 years	80.2 years
Hispanics	81.8 years	78.8 years
Blacks	74.7 years	71.8 years

When we look at this chart, several questions come to mind about the information provided. Where did the CDC obtain this data? Certain categories listed overlap, should they be considered individually? More specifically, are Hispanics and Black people included in the overall number, or should they be viewed separately?

Also, are Hispanics and Black people included in Men and Women groups? We do not know what information to accept from this chart because of the language. For example, we do not know what the category of Men means. Since the article provided no definition or explanation of the word Men, the reader has no idea of who that category included. We do know that all men are not the same and do not share the same lifestyle. So, we need to know the basics of the data source so we can make sense of the results. The same is true with the category for women which does not provide a definition or explanation. We need to know what women this group includes and the origin of the collected data. These questions are important if we are to accept the information the chart provides. Again, we know for certain that all women are not alike, nor do they share the same lifestyles. We might also question the reason if the last two categories include women.

The last two categories of Hispanics and Blacks underscore the language of race used in providing the chart information. The term Hispanics is a broad term that encompasses Spanish-speaking people and is used to identify ethnic groups. Therefore, even if someone is Hispanic, the reader has little information as to what that means relative to life expectancy. When terms are undefined or made unclear in their use, the information relative to them has no value.

The last category of Blacks raises the most questions since it also provides answers in its use. Obviously, the article views Blacks as an acceptable term to use in sharing information. However, Blacks are not defined or identified in any way. The article assumed that Blacks represent a black race of human beings and that they are alike in every way. Of course, we know that is not factual or scientific. So, why continue to use the word? In effect, the use of the word Blacks whether knowingly or not, reinforces the myth of European (white) supremacy.

We continue to accept the language of race in our daily lives as though it has no impact on the lives and well-being of individuals who come under constant scrutiny because of their complexion. One reason we continue to accept the language of race is that it appears truthful to us because it is used in science and sociology, along with statistics to garner our trust. Over the years, since the introduction of eugenics, we were led to believe that "there was a significant correlation between intelligence and cleanliness or a significant difference in criminality, fertility, or disease incident between people of different socioeconomic classes" (Nania, *AARP*). Since we know that numbers do not change, we usually accept them at face value which is precisely why they are employed to carry false information.

The most important concern we must have in considering whether language is objective or biased is based simply on its association with race, directly or indirectly. Any language that leads the reader to assume that biological differences among ethnic groups equal a different race is false and misleading. Our acceptance of any statistical information in language relative to race is false, damning, and dangerous.

CHAPTER 1

THE LANGUAGE OF RACE

When Amanda Gorman recited her poem at the inauguration of President Joe Biden she held the listeners captive with her words, voice, and message (Obama 75-80). Although we often take it for granted, language is an important part of who we are. Angela Carter said that "language is power, life and the instrument of culture, the instrument of domination and liberation. We can find no clearer words to express the essence of language. Carter's words ring true about language being the instrument of domination and liberation as well as culture when we look at America. Americans take immense pride in language, especially the written word, like in the Declaration of Independence, the Constitution, and the Pledge of Allegiance because of our emotional attachment to them.

Language in America has been a domineering instrument, controlling the lives of its citizens for better and for worse. While certain words, phrases, and thoughts can be inspiring, others can be controlling and enslaving. For example, the language of race has held America captive since its inception without segments of America realizing that they were being held captive. Society conditioned Americans to use and accept the language of race as something valid, ordinary, and normal because the government and all the social institutions were complicit in protecting it. We place a value on language based on who is using it and for what purpose.

The founding fathers knew the power of language and they knew that they wanted to protect and sustain their myth of supremacy and domination, so they invented a concept that would do both things simultaneously. The concept was the existence of subspecies of Homo sapiens, which meant that because they represented the species, all others would naturally be inferior to them. The words and the language would contain the concept of biological and/or genetic differences in the subspecies inferior to the species, thereby, ensuring their position of superiority and dominance over all human beings. The intention was to select a word and then construct a language around it to mask its actual intent—preserving and protecting the myth. The word selected was race because it was neither a fixed concept nor a defined one but could convey the impression of power to accomplish its mission.

The obvious power of the use of the word race or subspecies is multiple and simultaneous; that it, whenever the word race is employed, it does four things at once: unites, separates, discriminates, and controls. Equally important to the myth's wellbeing is that the continuous use of the word race and its derivatives constantly validates, perpetuates, and promotes its use. That is, whenever the word race or its derivatives are used in the language, it protects itself. For example, we hear on a regular basis the phrase "The Human Race" not realizing that no such thing exists. Race is a social construction not based on science or fact, but through continued use of the term, certain people accept it as legitimate. The appropriate phrase should be "The Human Species."

The language of race is so much a fabric of American society that people in general do not realize that it enslaves them. The irony of the phenomenon is that this language is a part of our lives and culture, but we never recognize it. For example, in all the federal legislation, especially those laws dealing with segregation and discrimination the one consistent word included is race. What that inclusion does is validates, perpetuates, and promotes the concept of races. If we wanted to prevent housing discrimination, we could simply say "there should be no housing discrimination," with no need for qualifiers such as race, gender, color, and other examples.

One of the ironies of the language of race is how it often makes the victim the villain for a variety of reasons. For example, individuals, groups, organizations, churches, companies, corporations, the government, and more have declared their battle against racism; they want to fight, to eliminate, and to destroy racism. These battles have been going on for over four hundred years and racism is still ahead and winning. Why? One would like to know how one fights a concept or myth. From the language of race, we would think that racism is the problem when in fact, it is the actions of people that accept the concept as valid and use that validity as justification to wreak havoc on the human population they see as different from themselves.

To show how the language of race is self-perpetuating, let us take the example of a person called a racist by another who thinks the term is an insult. In fact, the term racist serves not only to validate the acceptance of the concept of subspecies, but also to compliment the individual by acknowledging him or her as a member of the superior group. We continue to promote the usage of the language of race when we do not realize that we are doing so, and because we do not realize we are promoting the language through our usage of it, the language continues.

The language of race is so much a part of our everyday speech that we rarely recognize its power and influence in that we often use words and phrases that seem natural but carry the connotation of biological differences among ethnic groups. Depending on the context in which phrases are employed, a phrase like "you people" or "those people '' along with any number of combinations of people-related phrases can easily be interpreted by ethnic Americans as showing bias towards them. In the language of race, the underlying effect always emphasizes a biological difference among human beings.

Although the actual word race might not be employed, a substitute word or phrase is frequently offered in place of race. However, the replacement word or phrase always connotes a biological or genetic factor necessary to distinguish one group from another. The result is always the validation, perpetuation, and promotion of the myth of Anglo-Saxon supremacy and dominance. For example, society views the characteristic of intelligence as a valued element in the culture of ethnic groups. Therefore, the groups identified as having high intelligence, are viewed according to the method of measurement used to make that determination, as superior to groups that showed lower measurements. The key to recognizing the biased nature of the findings rests in the desire to associate the group differences on genetics or biology, not race.

Regardless of the language used, the effect is still to find something biological to use to contrast one group against another.

An article by Aubrey Clayton titled "How Eugenics Shaped Statistics" shows the importance of language and the power it can possess (*Nautilus*). The article's extended title underscores its focus "Exposing the damned lies of three science pioneers." The purpose of pseudo- science as far back as Morton was to protect, support, and promote the false concept of European supremacy by using science to ensure acceptance of whatever findings presented by representatives of science viewed with respect. The three pioneers in Clayton's article are Sir Francis Galton, Karl Pearson, and Ronald Fisher. What makes the work of these individuals important is that it is pseudo-science but accepted as legitimate by certain scientists even today.

The first of these pioneers is Galton, who was born into a prominent well-to-do English family. Charles Darwin was his half-cousin and the inventor of the theory of evolution. Galton used Darwin's theory of evolution and expanded it to include humans and as a result developed the idea that human characteristics were inherited and could, therefore, be acquired through breeding. This line of thinking led him to believe that through selective breeding of elite humans (Europeans) society would benefit. On the other hand, he believed that "breeding among those 'afflicted by lunacy, feeblemindedness, habitual criminality, and pauperism' [should be] discouraged. By being selective, like choosing the best traits of horses or cattle, he argued we could reshape the human species and create 'a galaxy of genius.'" Galton's objective to underscore the supremacy of the European expanded from this point.

Galton began a study collecting information about famous people in a variety of occupations and checked their family and relatives to determine the measure of success found in these families. Common knowledge tells us that the more wealth and affluence one has, the more likely the children will be provided with the opportunities to build on that success. This study resulted in a book published in 1869 called *Hereditary Genius* and indicated that natural characteristics could be expected or predicted from these famous people. One key factor was added to the findings as Clayton explained: "In a chapter called 'The Comparative Worth of Different Races,' he assessed that 'the average intellectual standard of the Negro race is some two grades below our own,' which he attributed to heredity. Galton expressed a frequent loathing for Africans, whom he called 'lazy, palavering savages.'" Clayton noted that Galton wrote a letter to the *Times* suggesting "the coast of Africa be given to the Chinese colonists so that they might 'supplant the inferior Negro race.'" The two glaring assumptions Galton passed along as facts were that an inferior Negro race existed and that heredity was responsible for human characteristics.

Today, Clayton indicated that "in the world of statistics, Galton is known as the inventor of the fundamental ideas of regression and correlation, related ways of measuring the degree to which one variable predicts another. He also popularized the concept that the spread of human abilities like intelligence tends to follow a normal distribution, or bell curve (an idea featured most prominently in the 1994 book, *The Bell Curve*).

Galton's work on the ranking of races was based on a normal distribution that became associated with applied statistics. Unfortunately, this work was instrumental in helping to introduce another false concept relative to eugenics: "in the 1840s, Belgian social scientist Adolphe Quetelet discovered the shape in the distributions of people's heights and chest sizes, leading him, with poetic flair, to imagine people as deviations from a common ideal, "the average man." From this point forward the theories begin to expand into complexities in that Galton had invented a scale with which to grade a variety of people, but an average could come only from people of the same race. For Galton, "the first hypotheses were taxonomic: whether individuals could be considered of the same species, or whether people were of the same race. The separation was everything— not how much, what else might explain it, just that it was there." For Galton, the protection and promotion of the myth of supremacy were that only the Europeans could represent the species. So, regardless of the separation or the degree of separation, any separation would accomplish the objective.

Galton's concept of eugenics provided a basis for finding differences among ethnic groups, and those differences could be employed to foster other theories relative to race. Joining Galton in the study of eugenics was Karl Pearson, considered an intellectual and prolific scholar. He graduated from Cambridge where he studied history, law, literature, physics, philosophy, and political science. He went on to become a professor of applied mathematics at University College where he met Galton. Sharing ideas of eugenics, the two men became collaborators. Pearson said eugenics was "the directed and self-conscious evolution of the human race,' which he said Galton had understood 'with the enthusiasm of a prophet'" (Clayton).

Pearson's views were extreme, ethnically biased political views and eugenics provided the platform for him to present and argue his views. Having invented the study of mathematical statistics, which he applied to science, Pearson believed that through controlled breeding inferior humans could be eliminated from the population. He noted in an address called "National Life from the Standpoint of Science," his view which he "called the scientific view of a nation— is that of an organized whole, kept up to a high pitch of internal efficiency by ensuring that its numbers are substantially recruited from better stock…and kept up to a high pitch of external efficiency by contest, chiefly by way of war with inferior races." He believed in race wars where the superior one would destroy the inferior one, thereby leaving only the physically and mentally superior humans.

We can readily see the limits to which pseudo-science would go to support and protect the myth of European Supremacy. Both Galton and Pearson never took the time to define race; they just accepted it and expanded the concept while knowing race had no actual basis in science. The idea of superior and inferior groups was promoted using science and mathematics which few seemed to question.

While Galton and Pearson promoted ideas of eliminating the inferior ethnicities of the world, a student of both Galton and Pearson, Ronald Fisher, was helpful in reconciling Mendelian genetics with Darwinian evolution, the project of evolutionary biology called 'modern synthesis.' He was well-known and celebrated for these and other contributions, then and now. In 2011, Richard Dawkins called him 'the greatest biologist since Darwin'. Like Galton and Pearson, Fisher believed in eliminating humans considered inferior stock. In the journal,

The Eugenics Review, Fisher wrote that "the nations whose institutions, laws traditions and ideals, lend most to the production of better and fitter men and women, will quite naturally and inevitably supplant, first those whose organization tends to breed decadence, and later those who, through naturally healthy, still fail to see the importance of specifically eugenic ideas." The concepts of what constitutes a superior group, and an inferior group are never described, but the reader assumes the model to be the European upper-class society.

Galton, Pearson, and Fisher conducted their work in the United Kingdom, but their efforts were not well-received or popular especially with religious institutions during the early 20th century. Their efforts were successful in achieving one piece of legislation, the Mental Deficiency

Act of 1913, which made it so anyone deemed "feeble-minded" or "morally defective" could be involuntarily committed. Because the standards for who qualified were notoriously vague, at one time there were upwards of 65,000 people living in such state-operated "colonies."

Fortunately, not everyone agreed with this act because it used eugenics as the basis for imprisoning people.

One person that objected to the act was G.K. Chesterton who identified eugenics as evil. He thought that ecumenists interfered in people's lives, "as if one had a right to dragon and enslave one's fellow citizens as a kind of chemical experiment." He recognized that eugenics was a pseudoscience based on nonstandard ideas or assumptions with little or no actual scientific backing.

Although eugenics did not gain wide popularity in the U.K., America offered a totally encouraging opportunity. The eugenic movement appeared in America, in part, by Harvard professor Charles Davenport who had studied Galton and Pearson's work. Davenport's work in eugenics added another dimension of influence found in American organizations. Like his professors, he favored selecting superior stock to populate the planet while reducing the number of inferior stocks. The supporting organizations were successful in lobbying for changes in American society in the twenties and 'thirties. These changes included "marriage prohibitions, restrictions on immigration, and forced sterilization of the mentally ill, physically disabled, or anyone else deemed a drain on society" (Clayton).

The power for influencing Americans to accept the concept of eugenics derived from the element of trust associated with science and mathematics or statistics. The problems created by eugenics and its use of statistics must be correct before statistics can be objective. The primary problem with statistics connected to eugenics is that it represents too few people of color within the population. Consequently, any conclusions drawn from data using science, statistics, and human beings, in general, would have to be suspect.

What we know from examining the work of Galton, Pearson, and Fisher is that they recognized only Europeans as representative of the species and all other ethnic groups as inferior. The ideal society would, in their estimation, exist with individuals just like them or as they described them-good stock. In any event, their collective purpose was to protect, preserve, and promote European supremacy using the language of race.

Anglo-Saxon Superiority Myths

When the English or specifically, the Anglo-Saxons came to America, one of the most important things they brought with them was a sense of superiority over non-Anglo-Saxon people. This sense of superiority was based on the idea of nation-group purity found in their ancestral ties to ancient figures who exhibited these qualities. That sense of racial superiority had served them well hundreds of years before coming to America and as they proceeded to build a new nation in America, it was to be the cornerstone of their self-image. What most people, including the Anglo-Saxons, did not know or acknowledge was the fact that their concepts of origin and race purity were all based on myths.

The primary source of the Anglo-Saxon myth came from a work by Geoffrey of Monmouth, *History of the Kings of Britain* which appeared around 1136. The book was recognized as the most "famous work of nationalistic historiography in the Middle Ages" (MacDougall 7). The historical account had the effect of "subduing the social animosities of the Bretons, Anglo-Saxons, and the Norman and drawing them together into a single nation." Geoffrey's work was a history of myths of national origins and associated the Anglo-Saxons with the Trojan origins. Unfortunately for the Anglo- Saxons the association with Troy proved to be false and therefore, exposed the myth as bogus.

The question of nation-group purity has always been a challenge for the Anglo-Saxons to maintain given the circumstances of the various historical events that affected the country. For example, the Norman Conquest as well as the former invasions of the Danes certainly had a biological impact on the country's population. Those events would challenge the nation-group and language purity of the Anglo-Saxons and put to flight the claim of superior origin, but not so with the Anglo-Saxons. They continued to view themselves as superior to the rest of the world despite the myth.

In the 1400s and 1500s, a shift in the Anglo-Saxon historical origin published information that indicated it had direct ties to Germany and showed the German language and character to be superior to that of the French. The extent of the myth of the purity of the German language was unwisely defended by Joannes Becanus (1518-1572), a Flemish physician that claimed that the German language was the language spoken in the Garden of Eden as well as being the language of the Old Testament. He went further to claim that all the languages originated from the Tower of Babel, except for the German language.

The widespread and varied stories of the myths of Anglo-Saxon superiority found support and/or rejection through the years by different historians and people of note. One such person of note that supported the myth or origin of the Anglo-Saxons having ties to Germany was Martin Luther. MacDougall noted concerning Luther that "As a devout Christian he accepted the biblical account of the origins of man, but saw Germans as first by right of their descent from Ashkenaz the first-born of Gomer, who through first-born descent from Japheth and Noe led back to Adam the father of the human race" (43). Luther was a strong German nationalist and supported the importance of the language. His statement underscored his belief: "I thank God that I am able to hear and find my God in the German language, whom neither I nor you would ever find in Latin or Greek or Hebrew." So, when the English associated their origins with Germany, they presented a picture of Germany and England having a common ancestry, even though that information was not factual, but mythical.

The newly formed connection of Germany with England invited an expansion of the supremacy myth to extend to all of Europe because Europeans viewed themselves as world leaders. The myth then became not only Anglo-Saxon supremacy but also European Supremacy. The European idea of superiority was not based on skin color although the Europeans realized they were different in complexion to their other compatriots. The basic differences, they assumed to be in character, intelligence, and culture expressively European that differed in the people they viewed as inferior. For Europeans, religion, especially Christianity, was a symbol of intelligence and civility.

Although the myth of European supremacy began in 1136 and was quite often debunked, the myth continued to grow and influence the thinking and actions of the Europeans. The pecking order of authority in Europe during the Middle Ages recognized the church and pope as supreme authority followed by the king and queen, prince, princes, and others, down to the peasant. Social value was not based on skin color, but on social, political, and economic status. The air of superiority and dominance by Europeans became vividly apparent through the actions of the European explorers.

For example, we can clearly note the actions of superiority exhibited by Christopher Columbus in 1492, when he reached the Caribbean Islands. His first order of business upon coming ashore was not to greet the inhabitants, the Taino Indians, but to claim the land and the people for the King and Queen of Spain. The writer Bartolome De Las Casas wrote an account of Columbus's action:

"All his life, Casas recalled how Columbus brought with him "seven Indians who had survived the voyage,' and 'beautiful green parrots… masks made of precious stones and fishbone… sizable samples of very fine gold, and many other things never seen in Spain" (Norton Anthology 5th ed. V1).

Casas described how the explorers, referred to as Christians, destroyed and depopulated Hispaniola and how "they began their subjection of the women and children, taking them away from the Indians to use them and ill use them." When some Indians tried to escape "the Christians attacked them with buffets and beatings, until finally they laid hands on the nobles of the villages. Then they behaved with such temerity and shamelessness that the most powerful ruler of the Island had to see his own wife raped by a Christian officer" (16).

The evidence of European attitude and behavior of superiority exhibited by Columbus and his men signaled the start of even more European activity. We learn that "in 1493, after reports of Columbus's discoveries had reached them, the Spanish rulers Ferdinand and Isabella enlisted papal support for their claims to the New World in order to inhibit the Portuguese and other possible rival claimants." That papal support came in the form of a treaty, the Treaty of Tordesillas which represented an agreement between Spain and Portugal that was meant to prevent conflicts over new lands. This agreement was accomplished when" the Spanish-born Pope Alexander VI issued bulls setting up a line of demarcation from pole to pole one hundred leagues west of the Cape Verde Islands. Spain was given exclusive rights to all newly discovered and undiscovered lands in the region west of the line" (Britannica). That meant Portugal had rights to the lands east of the demarcation line. However, the agreement also stated that neither Spain nor Portugal could claim any lands already belonging to a Christian ruler. That agreement to not claim any lands belonging to a Christian ruler was part of the understanding of the European supremacy myth.

Other European countries and even Portugal ignored the papal disposition and were not happy with it until it changed in 1506 with a new boundary. With the boundary change, Portugal was able to claim the coast of Brazil after its discovery by Pedro Alvares Cabral in 1500. Brazilian exploration and settlement far to the west of the line of demarcation in subsequent centuries laid a firm basis for Brazil's claim to vast areas of the interior of South America" (Brit. Jennifer Parnell).

Spain and Portugal were the first European countries to demonstrate their sense of superiority and power by exploring and colonizing other countries. However, other European countries quickly followed France, Netherlands, and England. Eventually, established slave-trade ports emerged along the coast of Africa by Portugal, France, the Netherlands, and England, with Portugal controlling the Atlantic slave trade. The Spanish brought enslaved Africans to Brazil to work the coffee plantations; they also established a major trade colony in the Philippines. The myth of European supremacy became firmly established between 1500 and 1770 by Spain, Portugal, England, France, and Netherlands through exploring, enslaving, and colonizing non-European ruled countries. Charles W. Mills summarized the consequences of European actions beginning with Columbus by noting that we live in a world which has been "foundationally shaped for the past five hundred years by the realities of European domination and the gradual consolidation of global white [European] supremacy" (*Racial Contract* 20).

Unfortunately, as American society developed Europeans and Americans held on to that myth of European supremacy although they know it to be false. They not only held on to the myth but found ways of expanding it and incorporating it into everyday life.

CHANGE ANGLO-SAXON TO EUROPEAN

The concept of Anglo-Saxon superiority constantly expanded in society because of the power and control it exerted over less powerful people or those people considered inferior in European society. The people viewed as inferior appeared to belong to a different race which served as justification for dominating and controlling them. The privilege of freedom became associated with whiteness and Europeans in general. The idea of freedom became an issue of who deserves to enjoy it. Tyler

Stovall wrote that "on the one hand was a freedom defined by savagery and subalterns; on the other was a set of natural liberties and rights owed only to adult white Europeans, whether they lived in America or in Europe." And so, the myth of supremacy expanded from the Anglo-Saxons to include the Europeans. Stovall noted that "As colonization and the Atlantic slave trade both expanded, they became even more integral to justifying the regimes of domination and violence erected by those republics in the pursuit of freedom" (*White Freedom*). The desire of the Europeans to show their superiority became more apparent through their behavior.

The move toward the concept of European supremacy became apparent when Spain started to colonize countries in the west and was followed soon after by other European countries. The countries targeted for colonization were all non-European and non-Christian. A philosophy of European (white) supremacy. One reason given for restricting the selection of countries to colonize is race. The significance of viewing race as a reason for the collective efforts of European countries to focus on non-European, and non-Christian was because it carried the myth of European supremacy. Mills goes as far as to state that the word race was never used in a political context regarding the ties between the Western countries. However, he noted that there has "been an unnamed global political structure—Global white supremacy..." (125). In effect, the tie that binds the European countries together is the belief in and the protection and promotion of the European supremacy myth through actions while avoiding the actual language of race.

Relocating to the North American continent did nothing to diminish the Anglo-Saxon view of themselves as superior to other peoples, but gave them the opportunity to enhance it. They lacked one essential element needed to support and promote their myth; something that they could incorporate into the very fabric of society. They got the opportunity to secure their myth by inventing a biological component they viewed as a subspecies based on the work of Swedish scientist Carl Linnaeus published in 1738 that identified all living matter, including Homo sapiens. The Anglo-Saxon myth, when viewed as biological, involved their inheritance of intelligence, character, and language along with a sense of superiority over other groups (races).

The key to the Anglo-Saxon myth enduring all these years and the subsequent invention of a subspecies called race is language. More specifically, when creative writers draft their stories, they usually invent the world inhabited by their characters. Along with the world, setting, and characters, authors also invent a language that serves to control the narrative, characters, and the society in which the characters live. For example, the world of *Harry Potter* is unique to Harry Potter as well as the language spoken in that world. Outside of Harry Potter's world the language spoken in that world would be meaningless in our real world. Although the Anglo-Saxons were not aware of the full extent of the power of language, they knew that it had the power to influence people. So, they chose language as their primary element of control and power over society.

The Anglo-Saxons chose the language of race to serve as the *sine qua non* of American society that gave them total power and control. The word race mirrors the concept of subspecies and whenever it is employed, it underscores the myth of Anglo-Saxon superiority as the only representative of the species, Homo sapiens. All other human beings, according to the myth, belong to a subspecies. So, whenever the word race is employed either explicitly or implicitly it supports the myth. In addition, when the word race is employed, it serves as a door into a society where the concept appears normal, and all the language that follows remains in that mindset or setting like that of the world of *Harry Potter*. More specifically, when someone uses the word race or it enters the conversation, the conversation will remain in the language of race with no way out except by avoiding the use of race explicitly or implicitly. The language used in *Harry Potter* makes no sense in our actual world, and so race and its concepts make sense only to those who accept it as valid. The word race captures the language whenever used because it protects itself, promotes itself, and perpetuates itself without the users realizing it.

Like race, racism after almost four hundred years still eludes people and organizations trying to defeat or destroy it. After all this time they have not come to the realization that they cannot defeat or destroy racism because it is a superstition and a concept. Racism became the supremacists' myth with the invention of a biological component they viewed as a subspecies based on the work, Carl Linnaeus, published that identified all living matter, including Homo sapiens. The Anglo-Saxon myth, when viewed as biological, involved their inheritance of intelligence, character, and language along with a sense of superiority over other groups (races).

A variety of scientific sources described the word race as a form of social construction. For example, an article by Dr. Gordon Hodson in *Psychology Today* noted in 2016 that "The fact that status plays a role in social categorization clearly demonstrates that categorization (e.g., as White, as Black) is a social construction. Many in the medical world offer the same opinion: "The genetic diversity that exists across the entire human race is very, very small, and race isn't even a good proxy for what diversity does exist. That's why we say race is a social construct: it's a human-invented classification system" (Center for Health Progress).

In addition to calling race a social construction we learn that "today, the mainstream belief among scientists is that race is a social construct without biological meaning. "Again, race is a social construction, where **societies generate informal or formal rules about what we see (i.e., perception) and how to act and treat others (i.e., discrimination)**" (*Scientific American*). Scientists do not characteristically recognize races as biologically meaningful. Angela Saini of *National Geographic* wrote that "although it has been known for at least 70 years that race is undeniably a social construct and that those 18th-century thinkers were misguided in the assumptions, many scientists still labor under the belief that race is biologically real." She added: "The story embedded itself so firmly that even when it became clear that we are one genetically indivisible human species, it remained difficult for many researchers to look beyond it" (16).

The reference to 70 years and the view of race as a social construction are for the benefit of non-scientists because the knowledge of race as invented to serve as a sub-species of the Homo sapiens goes back to the invention of taxonomy. The scientists knew that no subspecies of race was possible, but to promote the myth of European supremacy they promoted and protected the pseudoscience of race.

While certain people accept that race is a social construction with no scientific basis, they nevertheless continue to use the term as if it were legitimate. The fact that race is a pseudo-science term is the primary reason it exists. European supremacy depends on three areas of trust and believability to carry its message: science, statistics (mathematics), the Bible (Christianity).

CHAPTER 2
IMPORTANT PSEUDOSCIENCE PUBLICATIONS

In each of the following selections science and statistics, two trust-evoking subjects, are employed to promote the concept of European supremacy. The challenge is to have society accept the fact that race as a social construction causes no one to change their conception and use of it. The fact that race is a pseudo-scientific term should have been a cause for rejection, but in the selections that follow, we find that people constantly ignore the pseudo-science nature of race:

> "Human Biodiversity" is a euphemism that to lend respectability to their pseudo-scientific claim that white superiority has a genetic or evolutionary basis. Many white supremacist ideas derive from this claim: if white superiority is "natural" and immutable, there is no point in attempting to help non-white people whose inferiority is similarly "natural." Racist science also suggests that it is impossible for white people to live in harmony with non-white people, that society should (be

organized to give white people more power than other people, and that any demographic change that reduces the percentage of white people in a nation can only be detrimental to that nation's prosperity. (*Pharos*)

Various people believe that the idea of European supremacy began with Charles Darwin's book, *On the Origin of the Species* which introduced the theory of evolution. Although Darwin's book deals with plants and animals, not human beings, bigots at the time seized on the opportunity to use the concept of evolution to support their myth of European supremacy. Approximately ten years prior to the publication of Darwin's book, Carl Linnaeus had published his work on taxonomy that emphasized one species of human beings: Homo sapiens. The selections focusing on the third element, religion and the Bible, and follows the readings of the first two elements.

Systema Naturae by Carl Linnaeus

Carl Linnaeus, the "father of modern taxonomy", wrote one of the early works that influenced our understanding of plants and animals, over one hundred years before Darwin's book *Origin of the Species* (1858) and the concept of evolution. In this work, Linnaeus established a scientific system for naming and classifying living organisms that is still employed today. When Linnaeus established his system, it contained three kingdoms, classes, orders, genera, and species. His system included what came to be known as binomial nomenclature, the two words used to name all living organisms on earth. The term Homo sapiens, for example, takes the first word from the genus, and the second from the species. This system was important because at the time of the book's publication a variety of theories and beliefs concerning man's creation as well as his superiority or inferiority to other men.

In his system, "species represent groups that are set apart one from another and that will not produce fertile offspring when crossed." The term varieties used to indicate variations in the species, "show less distinct and less stable differences and do reproduce indefinitely by crossbreeding" (MacDougall 121). Because of this difference, MacDougall noted that Linnaeus divided the species *Homo sapiens* into four varieties with the following criteria:

Homo Americanus —Tenacious, contented, free — ruledby custom;

Homo Europaeus — Light, lively, inventive — ruled by rites;

Homo Asiaticus — Stern, haughty, stingy — ruled by opinion;

Homo Afer — Cunning, slow, negligent; ruled by caprice

(Barzun 45).

While Linnaeus's system was successful in furthering the knowledge of anthropology or ethnicity, it also presented scientific problems. For example, we recognize that each variety of man is usually represented by a geographical location as well as descriptions of their character and concept of governing. These characteristics were not based, according to Linnaeus, on biological differences; he saw these groups as being a part of the species. However, his descriptions invited speculation that each member of the groups possessed the same characteristics and therefore represented a fixed group. Are we to assume that all the inhabitants of the continent of Africa manifest the same characteristics? To assume the characteristics of each group fixed would be contrary to his concept of species.

We understand that each group of men belongs to the family of man, but what is the cause of the differences found among them? What Linnaeus identifies as varieties became the catalyst for people from all walks of professional life from scientists, scholars, clergy, doctors philosophers, and others to invent their own myth of races and to identify each one as being superior or inferior to the others. What these individuals did was an injustice to science. They began to promote the idea of biological differences within the species or invent a new species to justify their biases.

Barzun commented on Linnaeus's work: "In 1738 the Swedish savant Linnaeus gave his *Systema Naturae*, in which the species man stands at the top of the vertebrates and is divided into four races [varieties] with their physical and moral characteristics succinctly described." He continued by noting that "the eighteenth century gathered much new material from travelers and colonists all over the globe, and shortly the science of ethnology merged with natural history and incipient biology to form a new compound to which may properly be given the name of anthropology (*Race* 35).

Partly because of the biases held by a segment of the learned people of the eighteenth century as well as their desire to promote the concept of racial superiority and inferiority, they took liberties in interpreting Linnaeus's work. The concept of evolution had recently come into the area of science and presented a wide variety of ideas and concepts relative to race.

John R. Baker offered his view on Linnaeus by noting that "Linnaeus was so far from accepting the idea of equality among men that he listed the mental qualities of each race [they were actually called varieties] as distinguishing characters, comparable with the physical ones" (*RACE* 24). To highlight his point of Nordic superiority Baker said of Linnaeus that the Nordic people whom he grouped Under the name of *Europaeus* and described as "active, very acute, a discoverer." He further added to his show of biases by noting that "Linnaeus stigmatizes the section *Afer*, which is shown by his physical description to comprise the Negrid and Khoisanid races, [these last two names of races are Baker's invention] as crafty, lazy, careless."

McDougal noted that "elitist racial theories stressing Nordic superiority received further confirmation from the new sciences of ethnology and anthropology (in nineteenth-century usage the two terms were frequently synonymous)." He added that "beginning in the eighteenth century, pioneers like Swedish botanist Carl von Linnaeus, the French naturalist Comte de Buffon and the German physician

Johann Friedrich Blumenbach attempted to classify men principally on the basis of biological differences" (35). These differences did not at that time include skin complexion but focused more on geography, culture, and character.

Of course, the Anglo-Saxons and Nordics used the concept of biological differences among groups to support their myth and assume the title of the superior nation-group. The reference to the varieties which Linnaeus saw as part of the species changed surreptitiously to represent a subspecies for the purpose of justifying superiority biologically. The word invented by the Anglo-Saxons to secure, protect, and promote their myth of race.

Linnaeus's system has been a great contributor to our understanding of natural science as evident by its use in its expanded form today. Nevertheless, his work allowed for the invention of a variety of theories on races having biological differences all to maintain and promote the myth. Various methods were employed to protect the myth by finding physical elements primarily in African people of dark complexions or other people of color and focusing on these so-called differences to serve as proof of inferiority. Of course, the measuring stick was always the Anglo-Saxons and Nordics.

What the Anglo-Saxons also discovered by inventing a subspecies (race) and using the biased characteristics of the *Afer* group described by Linnaeus was that they could biologically justify enslaving Africans. Simply by using the word race, they could simultaneously cause nation-groups (ethnic groups) to unite, separate, control, and be discriminated against. In addition, the invention of subspecies (races) allowed the

Anglo-Saxons to assume the role of the only normal human beings and to view all other groups not only as inferior to them but also as monoliths.

Linnaeus's descriptions of the four varieties provided an opportunity for others to use the idea of subspecies to invent other theories. Regardless of the theories and approaches taken to discern differences among human beings, the primary objective has always been to show the Anglo-Saxon as representative of the species and all other groups as inferior or subspecies.

CRANIA AMERICANA SAMUEL MORTON

Once the false science of subspecies (race) became woven into the psyche of the European Americans, the Anglo-Saxons felt the myth of superiority and dominance was secure. One of the ways to ensure its maintenance and promotion was through publications by noted and respected individuals, especially men of science. One such individual was Samuel Morton, who at the age of seventeen attended lectures at the University of Pennsylvania Medical School. He earned his medical degree in 1820 and soon after joined the Academy of Natural Sciences of Philadelphia. After a trip to Europe, he established a medical practice in Philadelphia and became involved in the medical and scientific community. Morton's reputation in his community as a sophisticated and distinguished young doctor, no doubt, helped him in becoming a professor of anatomy at the Pennsylvania Medical College.

Morton's interest in Crania, according to Renschler and Monge, "may have originated in 1830 during his preparation for an anatomy lecture titled 'The Different Forms of the Skull as Exhibited in the Five Races of Men.' The reference to the Five Races of Men originated in the work of Johann Friedrich Blumenbach, a German scientist who also coined the term Caucasian in 1795" (Baker 26). Morton discovered that he lacked enough skulls to justify the identity of each race, so he decided to collect skulls from all over the world. Morton's collection of skulls, believed to be the most famous in the world, is in the University of Pennsylvania Museum Archaeology and Anthropology.

We understand that Morton's study of the skulls was not for the specific purpose of learning about skulls but to find justifications for not only identifying the so-called Five Races but also to protect and promote the myth of Anglo-Saxon superiority and dominance. Matthew Frye Jacobson noted that "the polygenist Morton declared in his *Crania Americana* (1839) that the "Caucasian' race was 'distinguished for the facility with which it attains the highest intellectual endowments." Because Morton was working with a pseudo-science all his conclusions relative to race and superiority would also be useless. For example, Nash and Weiss noted that Morton "offered white Americans presumably scientific evidence of the Negro's inferior mind. He had measured the cranial capacities of English, American, German, Chinese, Indian, and Negro skulls, and had discovered that the skulls of the whites had a larger cranial capacity than the skulls of the others. His conclusion was inevitable: whites were more intelligent." However, we note that the skulls of the whites Morton measured belonged to criminals that recently had been hanged. Subsequently, Thomas F. Gossett surmised that it "would have been just as logical to conclude that a large head indicated criminal tendencies." Nonetheless, European Americans wanted to believe the myth was real, and since certain segments of society constantly encouraged them, they came to accept it as real.

In America during the 1600s, color and later separate human creations came to represent the concept of race, and Morton's influence helped to promote these fallacies. Nash and Weiss noted that Morton's influential publication, *Crania Americana,* was based "on an acceptance of the diversity of men—the belief that there was not a single but rather many separate creations—and on the premise that the white race was biologically superior." Simply because Morton was established and respected in the scientific community, he was allowed to utilize a pseudo- scientific theory as evidence to support his conclusions. If he had not known the origins of the skulls beforehand, he would have had no way of differentiating them based on ethnicity, culture, or geographical location. Oklahoma City is home to a famous museum, The Museum of Osteology, which houses thousands of skeletons of creatures as small as a hummingbird to a whale. Among these skeletons are human skeletons. One display shows the human skulls of an infant, a teenager, and a mature adult. The exhibit did not include the identities of any of these skulls. At the base of this display is a printed statement that reads:

THE HUMAN RACE

Race has long been subject of debate and scrutiny. Biologically, race describes genetically divergent populations of humans. Race is also applied by anthropologists when studying the human species as well as forensic anthropology to aid in determining identities of skeletal remains.

Human skulls may exhibit various general characteristics that can aid in determining race, but these characteristics can vary between individuals, sexes, and geographic populations.

Having said all this, race has no real taxonomic significance. All humans belong to the same species, *Homo Sapiens*.

Somehow, time has a way of bringing the truth to the surface from whatever well the fallacy was resting. However, in Morton's time, segments of society accepted his conclusions because they wanted to believe in the myth of Anglo-Saxon superiority. Consequently, accepting race and subsequently, racism was a perfectly normal fact.

Diseases and Peculiarities of the Negro Race by Dr. Samuel Cartwright

In America's antebellum days, slavery was as common and normal as the sun rising each morning, but because of its importance to the economy and culture of the nation, it was a constant topic of concern. Various theories concerning the nature and origin of the different ethnic groups, especially the African or Negroes, relative to the Anglo-Saxons. Various aspects of these theories were promoted and published in books and journals and shared by word of mouth. The objective was always the same, to ensure the perpetuation and promotion of the myth of Anglo-Saxon superiority. Someone today reading an account of the thoughts and theories about the differences between the African American and the Anglo-Saxon might find the remarks humorous, but that would have been a mistake because regardless of how ridiculous the remarks might have appeared, they received thoughtful consideration.

One of the more influential people of his time was Samuel A. Cartwright. He was born in Fairfax, Virginia, in 1793, and later became a physician who practiced in the South, primarily Mississippi and Louisiana during the antebellum days. What made him influential was his theories relative to the slaves' minds, bodies, and environment and the impact those theories had on the slaveholders as well as the slaves.

An assortment of theories existed during the early 1800s about the origin of man, but two of those theories stood out among the others: monogenesis, the belief in one unified human race (species), and polygenesis, the belief that each race was created individually. Cartwright believed the latter and promoted his beliefs using pseudo-science as well as religion to convince others. His theories became popular because they fit well into the thinking of the day, but more importantly, perpetuated and promoted the myth of Anglo-Saxon supremacy. Rather than drafting a book describing his theories, we learned that The Medical Association of Louisiana asked Cartwright to investigate the diseases and physical conditions that were peculiarities of enslaved Africans. On March 12, 1851, Cartwright delivered his report as a speech, which was later published by the medical journal. Two elements of the speech that call attention to themselves are the sanctimonious quality of the speaker's tone as well as the apparent sarcasm in the words and their delivery that pictured the enslaved as ignorant, but trainable animals.

Slavery was certainly a common and everyday feature of society and discussions relative to the condition of the enslaved were not unusual, but Cartwright's characterization of the enslaved portrayed them more like animals rather than human beings. This characterization was common due to the view of the enslaved as non-human beings, but property. The sarcasm becomes apparent in his invention of the terms that described the so-called malady suffered by the enslaved.

In his speech, "Diseases and Peculiarities of the Negro Race" he invented a variety of terms to describe the actions and conditions of the slaves based on their behavior. The first term, Drapetomania, or the disease-causing Negroes to run away, he explained: "The cause in most of the cases, which induces the negro to run away from service [slavery] is as much a disease of the mind as any other species of mental alienation, and much more curable, as a general rule." He offered his assessment of a cure: "With the advantage of proper medical advice, strictly followed, this troublesome practice that many negroes have of running away, can be almost entirely prevented, although the slaves be located on the borders of a free state." In other words, the slaves wanting freedom and trying to escape suffer from a mental disease unique to the African American.

Cartwright's solution to curing this disease not only invokes concepts of the medical profession but also selective uses of the Bible and how they must be employed. In other words, he stated that God had created the negro to be submissive to the Anglo-Saxons and that the enslaved should be maintained in that condition and treated like children to keep them from running away. However, if they experienced Drapetomania, "they should be whipped to prevent them from running away."

Regarding the other disease, Dysaesthesia Aethiopica a disease that affected both mind and body, what he called Rascality, and viewed as partial insensitivity of the skin and "so great a hebetude of the intellectual faculties, as to be like a person half asleep, that is with difficulty aroused and kept awake." Cartwright invented these diseases that he called unique to the "negro race" and offered approaches to remedy them for the purpose of enhancing his reputation and appeasing his slaveholding audience as well as promoting the Anglo-Saxon supremacy myth.

Although Cartwright's work might appear absurd, the influence his theories had on medicine was not exclusive to the South, nor were they viewed as short-lived and relevant only for a brief period. In his essay,

"His Native, Hot Country: Racial Science and Environment in Antebellum American Medical Thought", Christopher D. Willoughby discussed how and why many of these myths are still with us today:

Historians of racial science have often focused on how polygenesis co-evolved alongside the emerging sectional crisis over slavery in the United States.6 Likewise, scholars of antebellum slavery and medicine have emphasized how medical knowledge about race was constructed on the ground, in the interactions among white physicians, white planters, and enslaved patients, with medical pedagogy occupying an ancillary role in the dissemination of racial theories.7 These works usually frame polygenesis and racial medicine as distinctly southern branches of knowledge, constructed under the exigencies of defending an unstable slave society. Building on works by these two groups of scholars, this essay argues that while slavery certainly played a key role in shaping the southern medical profession, medical schools in the North and South engaged in the production and distribution of racial theories. Moreover, during the antebellum period, the Medical Department of the University of Pennsylvania (MDUP) provided an important training ground for members of the American school of ethnology, including the movement's most prominent theorists Josiah Nott, Charles Caldwell, and Samuel Morton. Attending to medical education as a site for the proliferation of racial theories makes clear that the emergence of racial medicine in the antebellum era was as much the product of the professionalization of medicine as it was the story of recalcitrant regional politics. (330-331)

In addition, the record after slavery, of African Americans forced to serve as "guinea pigs" for medical science because of unfounded myths is long and continues to grow. Reports of those experiments include the research of Dr. J. Marion Sims, known as the "father of modern gynecology," who forced enslaved African American women, including Lucy, Anarcha, and Betsey to serve as his subjects and without the use of anesthesia. Also, the Tuskegee Syphilis Study indicated where African American men were deliberately given the disease and then observed as the disease manifested itself in them. These men received no medical assistance.

Certain aspects of the medical myths in existence today include the belief that African Americans are naturally immune to certain diseases, and that they have thicker skin and thicker blood than European Americans. The most held medical myth today regarding African Americans is they have a higher pain tolerance than their European American siblings.

The recent pandemic was instrumental in underscoring the gap between healthcare for European Americans and people of color. However, regardless of the plethora of information available concerning gaps in healthcare, we find that ethnic bigotry is neglected consistently as the topic in medical magazines and journals. An article in *Time* magazine called "Racism in Medicine" examined the subject in four leading medical journals and learned that "they almost never publish scientific articles that name racism as a driver of poor health outcomes. Of the more than 200,000 total articles published over the past 30 years in the *New England Journal of Medicine*, the *Lancet*, the *Journal of the American Medical Association*, and the *British Medical Journal*, fewer than 1% included the word racism" (Rhea Boyd et al. 29). The article added that over 90% of the scientific articles published were primarily opinion pieces and not studies or investigations.

The fact that most of the articles dealing with bigotry were not regarded as scientific but opinion was cause for the article writers to point out that "racism threatens and shortens lives. It is a public-health crisis. It is past time for the world's leading medical journals to name racism, publish evidence on how racism harms health and articulate how dismantling racism can prevent health inequities." The importance of the published word must not be understated, especially when those words directly impact the lives of human beings.

Slavery initially involved a variety of ethnic groups, the Indigenous people, the Europeans, and the Africans. When the slave trade began to focus on importing only enslaved Africans, the term slave was employed synonymously with Negros. The association of Africans with slavery is so common that today whenever the word slaves appears in texts spoken, most people associate the word Negro with it, even if the word appears in the Bible.

PREFACE THE ORIGIN OF SPECIES BY CLEMENCE ROYER (1862)

During the early years of the pseudo-science propaganda Campaign promoting race as real and legitimate, the chief players were all male, that is until Royer appeared on the scene. Born in France and homeschooled by her parents, Royer, described as an extraordinary nineteenth-century woman, was an anomaly for the time. Her association with the promoters of the pseudo- scientists is based on the work she performed in translating Darwin's Origin.

In 1862, Royer published her translation of Origin of the Species, which was well-received and brought her considerable attention. The attention was due to her insertions and "corrections" to Darwin's book. We learned that her Preface was a long and involved anti-clerical rant, as well as footnotes that challenged social thoughts and issues of eugenics and theories of race. Newitz noted that: "Though she was a fierce feminist who believed that women and men were cognitive equals, she didn't have the same beliefs about racial groups. In her Preface, she wrote that the races are 'not distinct species' but 'quite unequal varieties'" (*GIZMODO*). Royer's comments were not based on science, but her own ideas and opinions from reading and hearing the male proponents of race and the Anglo-Saxon myth of superiority.

According to Royer, "superior races are destined to supplant inferior ones...One needs to think carefully before claiming political and civic equality among people composed of an Indo-European minority and a Mongolian or Negro majority." Royer's comments like those of most promoters of race find themselves contradicting themselves in that she claimed that races are not fixed species but are unequal. She does not answer the obvious questions: How are the races unequal? What makes the races unequal? She, according to her male critics, did not fully understand the science, therefore, was not taken seriously.

Although her Preface on Darwin's *The Origin of the Species* was popular with the public, such was not the case with Darwin. An article in Scientific women.com noted: "Unsurprisingly, on reading Royer's 'translation' of Origin Darwin was perplexed to say the least; 'I received 2 or 3 days ago', he told Asa Gray in 1862, 'a French Translatior of the Origin by Madelle Royer, who must be one of the cleverest & oddest women in Europe'". What he meant by that statement was that "Royer… was an 'ardent Deist & hates Christianity & declares that natural selection & the struggle for life will explain all morality, nature of man, politicks &c &c!!!" (*Darwin Correspondence Project*). His displeasure with her treatment of his work was obvious.

In addition, Darwin in talking with Joseph Hooker mentioned that Royer's opinions were almost everywhere in Origin…when I express great doubt, she [Royer] appends a note explaining the difficulty or saying that there is none whatever! It is really curious to know what conceited people there are in the world." Darwin and his associates agreed that Royer's work was more of a hack job than a professional one, done by a female; and that it was written primarily for political purposes.

In an article by J. Harvey "Almost a Man of Genius: Clémence Royer, Feminism and Nineteenth-Century Science," we learn that in

1862, Édouard Claparède, who had a working relationship with Royer, wrote to Darwin and warned him "that he had tried but failed to prevent Royer from 'disfiguring your work completely.'" The thinking during this time regarding rewriting and politicizing someone's work "was not just bad scientific practice—it was also, and more importantly, a decidedly masculine way to behave." In other words, women were not to insert themselves in man's work, especially, in a scientific context as Royer had done. Women were to serve only as editors, proofreaders, and/ or translators.

Royer was not willing to accept the criticism relative to her acting like a man, so in 1874, she wrote and delivered a paper that addressed her thoughts and opinions regarding the criticism. In her paper, she criticized a male-controlled scientific establishment that directly showed a intolerance for women:

Up until now," she declared, 'science like law, made exclusively by men, has too often considered woman as an absolutely passive being, without instincts or passions or her own interests: as a purely plastic material capable of taking any form given her without resistance; a being without the inner resources to react against the education she receives or against the discipline to which she submits as part of law, custom or opinion. "Women," she concluded, "are not made like this."

Regardless of her work as a feminist, Royer still represents a promoter of the pseudo-science of race and supporter of the Anglo-Saxon and European supremacy myth. She took advantage of the opportunity to gain attention and recognition during a period when women were not generally valued in society and especially in science.

Inquiries into Human Faculty and its Development

By Sir Francis Galton (1883)

The myth of Anglo-Saxon superiority endured in the works of Sir Francis Galton, an anthropologist and explorer. His studies covered a variety of scientific subjects, but later in his life his research focused on eugenics and human intelligence. He was a precocious child and benefited from having a wealthy family that allowed him to be homeschooled. Charles Darwin, a cousin to Galton, in his book, *Origin of* the Species, introduced the theory of evolution which sparked an interest in Galton to focus his studies on human intelligence, genius, and selective mating.

Without question, Sir Francis Galton was the most influential orchestrator of pseudo-science for his generation and on. His work, rather than looking for physical differences from which to make an argument concerning ethnic differences, Galton focused on the inside to make his judgments and theories. During the nineteenth century, Galton was credited with popularizing the concept of eugenics. His work influenced our modern understanding of genetics; however, that understanding included examining the genetic backgrounds of people, primarily England's ruling class and determining what he considered good or bad traits. Once these traits became known, plans for marriage were employed based on what would constitute a good or successful marriage. Of course, the Anglo-Saxons were the models for people possessing good traits. Galton believed that specific characteristics found in segments of human beings could pass along through heredity. The essence of his work regarding eugenics, Judge found:

> In his brief definition, Galton laid out all the dimensions that came to characterize eugenics as an ideology and social/ political movement during the first half of the twentieth century. People had a firm trust in the methods of selective breeding as an effective means of improving the overall quality of the human species. There was a strong conviction of the power of heredity to directly determine physical, physiological, and mental (including personality) traits in adults. Whether ingrained or newly accepted there was an inherent belief in the inferiority of so races and superiority of others. This view extended to ethnic groups and social classes as well. A faith in the power of rationally applied science to solve pressing social problems. Science was turned to solve the intractable problems of urban and labor violence. The science of eugenics attempted to eliminate various forms of mental disease, including manic depression, schizophrenia, and feeblemindedness. ("Eugenics," Lora Judge, history.com 2002)

Like previous devotees of the pseudo-science of race, Galton accepted the concept of biological subspecies of human beings. He also used his biased knowledge to promote ideas regarding human beings superior and inferior mentally based on his acceptance of the Anglo-Saxon superiority myth. In his book, *Inquiries into Human Faculty* he wrote that: "Whenever a low race is preserved under conditions of life that exact an elevated level of efficiency, it must be subjected to rigorous selection. The few best specimens of that race can alone be allowed to become parents, and not many of their descendants can be allowed to live. He continued by noting that if a superior race was substituted for a low one, then the problems of inferiority would disappear. His next comments earned him his notoriety: "The most merciful form of what I venture to call 'eugenics' would consist in watching for the indications of superior strains or races, and in so favoring them that their progeny shall outnumber and gradually replace that of the old one" (199-200).

Galton saw eugenics as a form of animal breeding, but with human beings.

Galton's focus on intelligence attracted the attention of other scientists, especially the Frenchman Alfred Binet, a psychologist, who published the first standardized test of human intelligence in 1905. But it was an American, Lewis Terman, a psychology professor at Stanford, who thought to manipulate test takers' scores with their chronological age and arrive at a mental age or an "Intelligence Quotient" or IQ.

The lasting impact of the IQ is still felt today in a variety of ways. The IQ test became known as the Stanford-Binet IQ test and was first given to preschool children; Judge expressed concern for the detrimental effects of the IQ tests in this statement:

> The test used the basic technique of measuring intelligence mainly by asking vocabulary questions (synonyms, antonyms, analogies, reading comprehension). On the basis of IQ tests given to immigrants arriving at Ellis Island, eugenicist Henry H. Goddard "discovered" that more than 80 percent of the Jewish, Hungarian, Polish, Italian, and Russian immigrants were mentally defective, or feebleminded. Goddard believed

that such a defect was a condition of the mind or brain which is simply transmitted as a genetic trait. There was no attention paid to other factors that may have had a big affect on the test scores. Tests were all given in English and under a very strenuous environment to immigrants after traveled across the Atlantic Ocean. It would be impossible to rate real intelligence by using a test that is based on only verbal skills to someone in a language they were illiterate in.

Since the standard for IQ tests was based on the Anglo-Saxon population in America, most European Americans were viewed as normal. However, to control who among European Americans were considered normal, the science of eugenics was employed:

Eugenics was first embraced politically as a scientific means of halting the rising stream of "defective" immigrants who came to the United States from 1880 to 1914 seeking relief from the economic problems besetting Europe. These new immigrants arrived principally from Eastern and Southern Europe, the Balkans, and Russia and many were Jewish. These groups were ethnically and culturally distinct from earlier waves of foreigners, such as those in the mid-nineteenth century who had migrated mostly from Anglo-Saxon countries of Western Europe such as Germany, England, Ireland, and Scotland. To many Americans these new immigrants were considered "the dregs of humanity" and mentally deficient (as confirmed by tests such as those Goddard administered at Ellis Island), socially radical (many had been involved in trade-union activities in

Europe), and willing to work for low wages, thus taking jobs away from hard-working Americans.

Various detrimental experiences befell ethnic Americans because of the interest in eugenics, a pseudo-science of race invented by Galton, and the refusal of the promoters of it to acknowledge it as an invention to protect and promote the Anglo-Saxon myth of superiority.

The Rising Tide of Color Against White World-Supremacy (1920) by Theodore Lothrop Stoddard

The 1920s in America was a time that saw the nation involved in a variety of problems that had international interest. Both problems had to do with the concept of race, one focusing on the outside, the skin complexion, the other on the inside, focusing on man's genetic makeup. The problem of skin complexion was so serious that it triggered action from Congress that restricted the immigration of people from around the world. The Anglo-Saxons, European Americans were so concerned that America was losing its whiteness because of the various people entering America that Congress passed the Johnson-Reed Act "in 1924, President Calvin Coolidge signed into law the Johnson-Reed Act, which established a permanent race-based quota system for immigration to America. The law excluded those ineligibles for citizenship (that is, Asians and Africans)." In addition, the law changed the immigration process by moving the inspection from American ports to foreign ones. American demographics were changing too fast and not favoring the Anglo-Saxons, so the primary objective of this Act "was to restore the ethnic makeup of the country's white population to that of the early nineteenth-century. They planned to erase the demographic changes of the "new" immigration of the late nineteenth century from southern and eastern Europe" (Stoddard).

The Greek word "eugenic" meaning a good birth or origin became the focus of many at this time. The idea of eugenics was introduced by

Francis Galton in the late 1800s and fostered the notion that intelligence was hereditary. That idea led to his focusing on England's upper classes where he observed what he considered ideal traits. He believed that these traits could transmit down through breeding and could thereby improve humanity. The concept of eugenics arrived in America around 1900 and was immediately viewed as promising. Soon eugenics became exceedingly popular in America because Anglo-Saxon, European Americans believed that they had found a way to reproduce their human race—a master race. All this added information fed into the myth concept of European, Anglo-Saxon, European American race superiority and dominance.

Amid the excitement relative to eugenics a young man named Theodore Lothrop Stoddard, an American, also a journalist and a political scientist, wrote and published a book that captured the entire message of the Anglo-Saxon, European American myth. The book was based on eugenics and the pseudo-science of race. Stoddard was born in 1883, in Brookline, Massachusetts to American parents. He attended both Harvard and Boston University and later became an American historian, journalist, and political scientist. Stoddard wrote several books which advocated eugenicsand including (1920).

Stoddard was a firm believer in the myth of European supremacy and his actions and efforts in that regard are extensive. He was a member of the Ku Klux Klan, The American Eugenics Society, and a member of the organization founded by Margaret Sanger, the American Birth Control League, which today is known as Planned Parenthood. They believed in and advocated the concept of racial superiority and rejected ethnic mixing in marriage. His belief in racial purity was so strong that he did not care for immigrants coming to America who were not white. His definition of whiteness did not include all Europeans as well as people of color Mixing Anglo-Saxon, Nordic, and European blood with any ethnic group, he believed would weaken the white race. This mixing philosophy was stated by Stoddard's friend, Madison Grant, in the introduction to his book: "Democratic ideals among a homogeneous population of Nordic blood, as in England or America, is one thing, but it is quite another for the white man to share his blood with, or intrust his ideals to brown, yellow, black, or red men."

Stoddard did not limit his vision of European Supremacy to America but allowed it to encompass the entire planet. At one point, he laments what is happening to America: "Our country, originally settled almost exclusively by Nordics, was toward the close of the nineteenth century invaded by hordes of immigrant Alpines and Mediterranean, not to mention Asiatic elements like Levanican and Jews" (165). As a result of this immigration, he stated that " the Nordic native American has been crowded out with amazing rapidity by these swarming, prolific aliens, and after two short generations he has in many of our urban areas become almost extinct."

The growing migration within America of what Stoddard and others considered lower type humans caused trouble for the Nordics. He noted that "such migrations upset standards, sterilize better stocks, increase low types, and compromise national futures more than war, revolutions, or native deterioration" (308).

Stoddard's popularity faded after World War II, but during the 1920's he was so popular that his book was mentioned in the novel, *The Great Gatsby* (1925) not by the official title, but one that people familiar with the book would recognize—*The Rising Tide of Color*. The novel, *The Great Gatsby*, is an example of Stoddard's rejection of ethnic mixing or the adulteration of the Nordic race by lesser humans. The female character Daisy is a Nordic, but Gatsby is not, so the chances of Gatsby not winning Daisy's heart is a foregone conclusion.

In 1929, Stoddard had the misfortune to debate the noted African American historian, W.E.B. DuBois in a setting with a mixed audience. The event turned out to be a disaster for Stoddard who became the butt of a joke about racism. *The Chicago Defender* newspaper reported Stoddard as saying: "The more enlightened men of southern white America are doing their best to see that separation shall not mean discrimination; that if the Negros have separate schools, they shall be good schools; that is, they have separate train accommodations, they shall have good accommodations. [laughter]."

The report continued: "Du Bois, in responding to Stoddard, said the reason for the audience's laughter was that he had never journeyed under Jim Crow restrictions. 'We have.' Du Bois told him and the mixed audience."

Stoddard's work always carried with it the desire to protect and promote the myth of European supremacy because he passionately believed in the concept of biologically different races. At one time prior to 1924, Stoddard realized that the Nordic population was decreasing so he decided to add the "lesser whites" to the number of whites, but not as whites, but as Caucasians. Certain immigrants from various parts of Europe were frequently identified as Negros, like, for example, Italian, Jewish and Mexican people to mention a few. Stoddard maintained that "the melting pot may mix but does not melt." He saw each ethnic group as biologically different from one another. However, among the different whites he maintained that "differences granted, there must be *some* sense of a shared race solidarity, pride, and destiny among Nordics, Alpines, and even Mediterraneans" (Jacobson 97).

Coming of Age in Samoa: A Psychological Study of Primitive Youth for Western Civilization by Margaret Mead (1928)

Like C. Royer, Mead was a young woman with an interest in science whose work was not readily accepted by her male counterparts. Mead was born in Philadelphia, Pennsylvania in 1901, the first of five children born to Edward Sherwood Mead and Emily Fogg Mead. Her father was a university professor of finance, and her mother was a sociologist, so they valued education in their home. Mead earned a bachelor's degree from Barnard College in 1923; she continued her education at Columbia University where she earned a master's degree in 1924 and her Ph.D. in 1929. Her studies at Columbia University involved an association with professors Franz Boas and Ruth Benedict, both noted anthropologists.

During her formative years, Mead lived in an America that focused attention on the effects of the myth of European supremacy. Emphasis on the ideal family as having a European heritage as well as physical features of blond hair and blue eyes were part of a campaign to view them as normal. Shortly after Mead entered Barnard College, concerns about immigration had risen to such a point that two congresspeople wrote and passed a law known as the Johnson-Reed Act. The law was enacted in 1923 and would have caught the attention of Mead and her professors. The law focused on Asians and prevented them entry into the United States. In addition, the law established quotas for the number of immigrants from the Eastern Hemisphere entering America. Furthermore, the law provided control of the funding and the enforcement necessary to uphold the ban on other ethnic groups wanting to immigrate to America. So, while the ideal view of America was that of a democracy, the reality was that it was a European American society with biases against people of color.

Mead should have been mindful of the Supreme Court finding in Thind v. United States in 1923, and its definition of American citizenship a year before earning her master's degree from Columbia University, because the court contradicted the thinking that it had ruled on back in 1912, Ozawa v. U.S. In the Ozawa case, Ozawa was applying for citizenship in America, but the court found that he was not ineligible because he was not white. The court defined someone white as someone belonging ethnically to a group with Aryan or Caucasian heritage. Ozawa could not claim either of these ethnic identities as belonging to him, so he lost his case.

However, Thind appeared before the court and showed evidence that he possessed both elements of Aryan and Caucasian heritage and as an Asian Indian was considered Caucasian and therefore white. The court ruled that because he did not look white, he was not white even though he met the criteria the court had previously used in the Ozawa case. In effect, the judge suggested that to be white a person must have the physical characteristics of Europeans.

The court's finding not only supported the myth of European supremacy but also the false concept of biological differences among ethnic groups. As a young and aspiring anthropologist, Mead showed an interest in the differences between Western and non-Western cultures.

So, in 1925 she went to live, study, and do field work in the Samoan Islands. She knew that to gain genuine insight into the culture, living among the Samoans and learning their language would be necessary. Rather than try and observe the entire population, Mead focused her attention on young adolescent girls and followed the cultural practices, habits, attitudes, and lives in general through puberty. Her objective in going to Samoa was to answer the question: "Are the disturbances which vex our [Western] adolescents due to the nature of adolescence itself or to civilization? Under different conditions does adolescence present a different picture?" (6-7). Her answers to those questions came in her report published as the book *Coming of Age in Samoa: A Psychological Study of Primitive Youth for Western Civilization.*

The book was published in 1928, and subsequently, it created quite a controversy as Newitz explained: "Mead's famous work of anthropology is an example of scientific racism that explores racial differences through the 'noble savage' stereotype rather than the 'dumb savage' stereotype that haunts the work of everyone from

Galton to Wade." The reason for the controversy surrounding Mead's work is that it contradicted the European (white) supremacy myth. Newitz continued by noting that Mead "while there, [in Samoa] she became convinced that their 'simple' way of life was superior to that of 'civilized' people in Europe and the Americas." Mead further "described the sexual openness and communal culture of the Ta'u as a kind of beautiful innocence and argued that American culture had become unhealthy because it had suppressed a more primitive way of life." Of course, in America during this time any word or work that detracted from the myth of European supremacy was unacceptable and received considerable negative criticism.

Mead in a subsequent publication of her book commented on what she tried to do and how American society received what she did. The concept of culture as a factor in the lives of individuals was a new concept. She noted that "the idea that our every thought and movement was a product not of race, not of instinct, but derived from the society within which an individual was reared, was new and unfamiliar." What Mead noted in 1973 relative to the myth of European supremacy based on the concept of race and culture was that the bias remained: "But the renascence of racism among some scientists and the pleas for a harsh manipulative behavioralist among some psychologists make me wonder whether the modern world understands much more about the significance of culture" (x-xi).

The primary characteristic of Mead's work that places it in the pseudo- science class is her acceptance of race as a valid concept relative to the variety of ethnic populations. However, she attempted to show through her work that race received too much emphasis.

RACE

BY JOHN R. BAKER (1974)

John Randal Baker was a firm proponent of the myth of European supremacy and joined with other like-minded men to influence and promote the myth. Baker was born in 1900 to British parents–Rear-Admiral Julian Baker and Geraldine Eugenie. He was the youngest of five children. His education included a bachelor's degree from New College in Zoology and subsequently a Ph.D. from the University of Oxford, in 1927 in biology. According to his writings, his interests centered around finding scientific evidence to support the theory of European Supremacy.

In his book *RACE,* he sought to find evidence of ethnic inferiority in people of color, especially people of African descent. He found some forms of satisfaction relative to his views "by reviewing the historical views about racial equality of such persons as Rousseau, Kant, Hume, Voltaire, and others. He shows by direct quotation that each of these thinkers, many of whom were irreligious and 'progressive' in their politics, believed in the inequality of races in general and the interiority of the Black" (Book Reviews: Science, Racism and Social Darwinism, Sage Journal). Baker believed that the support of these thinkers added credibility to his belief in the myth and that using the social construct of race was the correct approach to justifying it.

The topics of race and immigration in the early 1920s were not just an American concern. We learn that "in the United States race and immigration have been important issues, whereas in Great Britain the relationship between heredity, social class, and inequality was of greater concern" (Kenny). So, while the efforts in America involving eugenics focused on physical or observable ethnic characteristics, Baker and his British colleagues focused on intelligence, heredity, character, class, and race. Baker's book *RACE* promoted the thesis that "African Americans have proportionally fewer such people [people with high IQs etc.] than more favored 'races' and therefore that their place—as a statistical group—would naturally fall closer to the bottom of the meritocratic class hierarchy, even in an environment of equal opportunity." His philosophy relative to this thesis is that the more people representing this lower group on the planet, the dumber the planet becomes. As Kenny put it, "[t]he long-term fate of a given segment of the general population would be determined by the relative number of talented high-IQ people within it, coupled with a tendency of like to mate with like."

Baker's idea of the top IQ people ruling society was not viewed by various scientists as acceptable without scientific proof. A segment of American scientists took the idea and expanded it. For example, in 1994 a best-selling book appeared called *The Bell Curve* that made questionable claims relative to race, heredity, and class. These claims shared similarities in genetic references present in the writings and work of Baker in his book *RACE*. In characterizing the recent claims of genetic superiority Baker found in Europeans, Kenny again noted that "*The Bell Curve* combined genetic fatalism, a conservative anti-interventionist political stance, and solicitude for the biologically less fortunate."

A recent article on Baker's book *RACE*, the author goes to great lengths in describing the work and its various aspects of it that lend themselves to examination. The article, "John R Baker's *RACE*: 'A Reminder of What Was Possible Before the Curtain Came Down'" suggests that the work done by Baker provided a variety of possibilities for support of the myth of European (white) supremacy until the results of the Gnome project became known and published. The science writer Marek Kohn noted that "Baker's treatise, compendious and ponderous, is possibly the last major statement of traditional race science written in English" (*The Race Gallery*). Of course, he was incorrect since we have seen two similar works published in the United States: *The Bell Curve* in 1994 and *A Troublesome Inheritance* in 2014. Both of which attempt to make the claim of genetic superiority in support of the European supremacy myth. One of the primary problems with Baker's book, according to Michael Kenny, is a lack of credible and dated evidence. It noted that "Baker's omission of genetic data means that, unusually for a scientific work, in the material he does cover, *RACE* scarcely seems to have dated at all. This is because the primary focus of Baker's book—namely, morphological differences between races is a field of study that has become politically suspect and in which new research has now all but ceased."

Another recent article on *RACE* by Michael Banton (Book Reviews, University of Bristol, 1974) recognizes early on that Baker's intention is the selective use of material and date to foster his idea of European supremacy by using genetics to underscore so-called racial differences. Of course, we know that genetics does just the opposite regarding Homo sapiens. Banton opts out of reviewing the subspecies history because he sees it as not up-to-date and deficient in various instances. He stated that while the work, in general, is unsystematic and unsatisfactory, there are many and more serious problems with "the book's scientific pretensions." More specifically, Banton noted that "what Baker chooses to include and what exclude is often governed by personal whim and happenstance. There is no reference at all to animal behaviour studies though they are very relevant to the study of raciation." He further commented about how Baker plays with language to try and underscore his objective.

Finally, Banton expressed disappointment relative to Baker's book. He noted that while Baker writes about how genetics underestimate the difference among taxa, he never makes an argument relative to an understanding of race made by genetics. He concluded that "in my view this work contains some alarmingly poor science...I believe that it reflects great discredit on those responsible for its publication." Regardless of the expressions offered by scientists today, when Baker published his first book, certain scientists thought it was revolutionary and a contribution to the field of anthropology. Among the people that praised his book, René Dubois concluded that "[w]ith Professor Baker's book we have at last a compendium of biological facts about the various groups of men—a compendium which can provide a factual basis for discussion of racial differences."

The comments of Arthur R. Jensen provided more creditability to Baker's book in the eyes of some like-minded people: "A most impressive display of profound scholarship and vast erudition in every aspect of this important topic. Recent studies of racial differences in cognitive and behavioral characteristics have generally overlooked or belittled the biological, anatomical, physiological and evolutionary lines of evidence." He added that "Baker provides the essential basis upon which any objective, rational, and scientific discussion of racial differences must proceed." In other words, Jensen viewed Baker's book as the evidence necessary to prove the supremacy of the Europeans or European Americans.

When we remember that the consistent objective of all the pseudo-scientists is the preservation and promotion of the European supremacy myth, we also realize that they employ a variety of approaches to meet that objective. In every case, the individuals involved in this venture have never defined race, although they have referred to certain ethnic groups as subspecies, but even then, no evidence to support their contentions existed except in the form of the information Baker presents. That information is based on the false concept of race.

Baker was a staunch believer in one of the most irrational myths accompanying that of European supremacy, the belief of African Americans viewed as possessing a fraction of their genetic make-up from European Americans. During slavery and afterwards, African Americans that were the product of a European American and African American were called mulattoes which were viewed as the mathematical equivalent of 50% of each parent. Names were given for other African Americans with lesser amounts of European American ancestry. For example, an African American considered to have 25% European American ancestry was called a quadroon; for 1/8 %, the name was octoroon. This naming process was done during slavery to increase the value of the enslaved. No one published any evidence or data on how or what qualified a person as a full-blood European American or African America.

Baker believed that genetics and inheritance played a part in character and intelligence with respect to African Americans. He found others who believed as he did and quoted from their works.

He noted that A.H. Stone wrote that "[p]ractically all the so-called Negroes of distinction are not real Negroes at all…. There can no longer be a question as to the superior intelligence of the mulatto over the Negro" (*RACE* 504). To support his claim, he listed four African Americans of note and underscore that their ancestry included European Americans. Included in the list were Dr. W.E.B. DuBois, Charles W.

Chesnutt, H. O. Tanner, and Booker T. Washington. Baker does provide various pictures of certain mixed-blood African Americans, but at no time or in no place are definitions for bloodlines provided. The primary assumption of European Americans representing superior human beings underlies the purpose of the study and, indeed, the book.

The Bell Curve: Intelligence and Class Structure in American Life (1994)

Appearing in 1994, *The Bell Curve: Intelligence and Class Structure in American Life* by Richard J. Herrnstein and Charles Murray was heralded by Michael Novak from *The National Review* as nothing short of phenomenal: "Our intellectual landscape has been disrupted by the equivalent of an earthquake." This controversial *New York Times* Bestseller brought with it both praise and criticism because of the information about race the writers attempt to present as valid. Their initial mistake in their research is to substitute intelligence for race, so they did not have to use race as the focus of the work. Nonetheless, when they make references to the intelligence of blacks and whites, the meaning is still about race.

The purpose of the work is to validate, perpetuate, and promote the myth and concept of European, Anglo-Saxon superiority and dominance over all other human beings. Intelligence is considered a relative term that depends on the people, place, and culture that educates their world. So, people from rural communities would not be expected to reflect a high degree of knowledge about life in an urban community. However, these writers went to the work of Sir Francis Galton to establish intelligence criteria "by using the great families of Britain as a primary source of data. He presented evidence that intellectual capacity of various sorts ran in families in *Hereditary Genius,* published just a decade after the appearance of *Origin of Species* in 1859." Of course, Herrnstein and Murray noted that: "So began a long and deeply controversial association between intelligence and heredity that remains with us today." In other words, if intelligence is inherited, then it is genetic and biological which allows the assertion of a human group with superior intelligence and groups with lesser intelligence.

If the writers had restricted their work to science, their findings might be perceived as having merit, but when they venture into the language of race their credibility becomes questionable. One critic noted that the writers talked mostly about blacks and whites and noted further that "[b]ecause many studies show that IQ is a strong indicator of economic success, they [Herrnstein and Murray] believe that IQ differences are at the root of racial differences. They use 'scientific' data about IQ scores to dismiss the idea that political inequalities and the history of slavery in the

U.S. are causes of racial inequality" (Nimitz). In addition, the writers make unfounded assumptions about ethnicity when they assert that "[l]large human populations differ in many ways, both cultural and biological." Their pandering continues with the use of unidentified tests and other data.

The use of the language of race and its cause for questioning the information it contains became obvious when the writers mixed their references: The difference in test scores between African Americans and European-Americans as measured in dozens of reputable studies has converged on approximately one standard deviation for several decades. One can notice that the terms African Americans and European-Americans were used in that part of their statement. The second part of the statement stated that: "Translated into centiles, this means that the average white person tests higher than about 84 percent of the population of blacks and that the average black person tests higher than about 16 percent of the population of whites." What can the reader gather from the writers' comments?

Their statement mentioned test scores from reputable studies, but no studies were named, so we have nothing to check for accuracy. The terms African American and European-American are employed, but not defined, and that is important because they were not used continuously but substituted with the terms black and white. So, both populations of blacks and whites became monoliths with no individual differing characteristics within each group. At each juncture throughout the book where the authors want their findings to support the myth of Anglo-Saxon supremacy, the element of race enters the process and brings it into question.

In Chapter 13, the authors make their point relative to race, IQ, and genes by listing three conclusions they reached. The first conclusion stated that "[a]ll races are represented across the range of intelligence, from lowest to highest." A definition of race has yet to be produced, so how one establishes a ranger of intelligence, must be of concern. The second conclusion noted that "American blacks and whites continue to have different mean scores on mental tests, varying from test to test but usually about one standard deviation in magnitude—about fifteen IQ points." Again, one must question the origin of the tests and their context since we know that differences in education, income, housing, health, and a host of other things are at play in assessing one's intelligence. Finally, the third conclusion stated that "[m]mental-test scores are generally as predictive of academic and job performance for blacks as for other ethnic groups.

As far as the test being biased at all, they tend to overpredict, not underpredict black performance" (562). When the language of race is used, we are supposed to accept it at face value, not questioning its origin or validity.

For example, in Chapter 19, "Affirmative Action in Higher Education," the writers try to convince the readers that Affirmative Action is bad for African American students because their intelligence level is well below the average European American student. That being the case, the entire institution of higher education suffers from the downward drag of the low ability of African Americans. They noted that "[o]n elite campuses, the average black freshman is in the region of the 10th to 15th percentile of the distribution of cognitive ability among white freshmen. Nationwide, the gap seems to be at least that large, perhaps larger." So, the implication from the writers' remarks is that no African American students should be admitted to colleges and universities because their low intellectual abilities will pull the institutions down.

The writers' argument throughout the book is that to have a great society we must place more interest in those people with higher intelligence. "Much of public policy toward the disadvantaged starts from the premise that interventions can make up for genetic or environmental disadvantages, and that premise is overly optimistic." They continued by saying "[m]uch can and should be done to improve education, especially for those who have the greatest potential" (550). In other words, society needed to provide an adequate opportunity to those with high IQs which would lift the entire society. Although they proposed to focus on the individual rather than the group, their findings inferred that those individuals with the high IQs belong to one group—European

American. Milton Friedman said regarding this book "[t]his brilliant, original, objective, and lucidly written book will force you to rethink your biases and prejudices about the role that individual difference in intelligence plays in our economy, our polity, and our society." Thomas Sowell said that "[t]his is one of the most sober, responsible, thorough and thoughtful books to be published in years. I don't happen to agree with everything in it, but that is beside the point." One cannot read this book without recognizing the argument made by the writers from the beginning- that intelligence should be the key element in society that determines privilege and supremacy. With that in mind, the book moved to establish the Anglo-Saxon or European American or white group as having the highest IQ of all the groups. Consequently, the book exchanged race for intelligence and in so doing made the case for validating, perpetuating, and promoting the myth of European and European American supremacy. In an article in *The Contemporary Heretic*, the writer offered two statements that are essential to understanding the problems in using race as a factor relative to IQ:

1. High intelligence causes upward social mobility

2. A privileged upbringing causes higher intelligence

The focus of each of these statements has little to do with race per se, but more with economics, education, and social class. That is, children raised in the same home with the same parents will not all have the same IQ, so biology and heredity do not necessarily promote higher intelligence or upward social mobility. Although higher intelligence and social, and economical status can impact a person's future potential, neither is based on the race of the individual.

Again, the fact that studies using race as an acceptable scientific concept promote ideas of superiority and inferiority based on relative elements simply adds to the collection of pseudo-science that fails to justify or prove the existence of an inferior subspecies of humans.

Battle Hymn of the Tiger Mother by Amy Chua (2011)

The social conditioning of the race myth impacted all Americans regardless of their ethnicity and the acceptance of the myth directly influenced their behavior whether they were cognizant of it or not.

For example, one of the popular books written in 2011 by an American woman of Chinese ancestry described in extensive detail how she raised her two daughters in America but rejected what she considered the "American" idea of child-rearing. The book, *Battle Hymn of the Tiger Mother by Amy Chua.*

The book received a variety of reviews that commented on Chua's child- rearing: "[f]ascinating...The most stimulating book on the subject of child rearing since Dr. Spock" *(Seattle Post-Intelligencer)*. *The New York Review of Books* commented in greater detail that "[t]he analogy of child-rearing to our national situation is clear enough: just as American parents are too concerned with 'self-esteem' without basing self-esteem on an actual accomplishment...so our entire culture operates on some notion of natural rights that is no longer realistic. Chua's point is that a delusional culture based on unearned self-esteem can't for long be a realistic player in global competition for influence, power, and resources." Chua's attitude and actions relative to child-rearing underscore the stereotypical concepts of ethnic group superiority and inferiority by pitting Chinese culture versus Western culture. American culture and Western culture are assumed to be reflected in the lives of upper-middle class and above European American (white) citizens; they represent the standard Chua uses as her guide to success. If she can exceed the Western standard, then she can view her actions as being successful.

In her comparison of Chinese and Western cultures, Chua describes three cultural things that give Chinese mothers an advantage over Western mothers when it comes to child-rearing. Although she does not state it, she implies that these differences might be more biological than cultural or a combination of both when she says that Western parents are extremely anxious about their children's self-esteem. They worry about how their children will feel if they fail at something, and they constantly try to reassure their children about how good they are notwithstanding a mediocre performance on a test or at a recital." Chua's concern is always on competition where her children must be number one or the best and assumes that Western mothers are not as concerned. She noted that "Western parents are concerned about their children's psyches. Chinese parents are not. They assume strength, not fragility, and as a result they behave differently" (52).

The second thing Chua mentioned was that "Chinese parents believe that their kids owe them everything. The reason for this is a little unclear, but it's probably a combination of Confucian filial piety and the fact that the parents have sacrificed and done so much for their children." Her statement is again confusing because she talks about what the parents believe about their children and she bases that belief on philosophy or culture. She writes about how engaged and involved Chinese mothers are in their children's lives and "that Chinese mothers get in the trenches, putting long grueling hours personally tutoring, training, interrogating, and spying on their kids." In return for their mothers' efforts the children must "spend their lives repaying their parents by obeying them and making them proud" (53).

The third element in Chinese children-rearing is the parents' belief that they know what is best for their children "and therefore override all their children's own desires and preferences. That is why Chinese daughters cannot have boyfriends in high school and why Chinese kids cannot go to sleep-away camp." She defends the actions of the Chinese parents by underscoring that they care deeply about their children and would sacrifice anything for them. Chua admits that this parenting mindset is not exclusive to the Chinese, but also practiced in countries like Korea, India, and Pakistan.

Throughout her book, Chua constantly compares Chinese culture to Western cultures that she holds in high esteem because her parenting style competes with Western culture child-rearing models. One reason for her approach to child-rearing appears to involve her concept of social values and competition since she wants her girls to always be number one, or the best in all their educational endeavors. Why? One impression is that being number one or the best in the class removes the element of inferiority based on ethnicity. While she underscores the benefits of Chinese culture in child-rearing, she is also attempting to debunk the stereotypes associated with Chinese and Asian people in general. All while she and her family live in an upper-middle-class environment in a large metropolitan city in America.

One of the most obvious differences between Western culture and Chinese culture from Chua's perspective is that Chinese parents prepare their children for a future the parents see as necessary while Western parents "respect their children's individuality encouraging them to pursue their true passions, supporting their choices, and providing positive reinforcement and a nurturing environment." The Chinese parents work towards arming their children "with skills, work habit, and inner confidence that no one can ever take away" (63). Chua avoided the subject of ethnic groups and their stereotypical characteristics directly, but her actions underscore her challenge of those characteristics for Chinese and Asian people. She also avoided mentioning the fact that Western society invented the human characteristics viewed as superior or inferior to ethnic groups. In Western society, self-esteem was discouraged and frowned upon for people of color.

Chua's book clearly showed the influence of the concept of race and Newitz noted that "[t]hough she doesn't explicitly describe the difference between Chinese and Americans in genetic terms, she does a kind of pop sociological analysis that suggests Chinese culture is superior and explains why Asian kids often succeed while their Western counterparts become aimless flakes." Chua's actions throughout her narrative show her constant battle between Chinese and Western cultures. Why does she believe her daughters must be top students in all their endeavors? The suggestion is that while she knows the myth of European supremacy is prevalent in American society, if her daughters' achievements can succeed those of American girls, then that tells her that her Chinese culture is comparable to the best in America.

In other ways, Chua shows a competition between Chinese culture and Western culture. For example, she marries an American man. She has her daughters study under the best Western professionals in their quest for superiority. If these actions do not suggest a challenge of cultures, then why not marry an Asian man, and why not have her daughters study under Asian musical greats? The point is that Chua reveals in her words and actions a belief in cultural superiority and inferiority as represented in Chinese and European cultures and that biology, regardless of the degree, plays a part in determining one and the other. Her efforts suggest that she views her Chinese culture as superior to European American culture. That is why she uses her Chinese culture in raising her daughters.

The comments by Kurt Vonnegut show a contrast to the teaching methods and attitudes associated with competition, success, and failure for children and subsequently as adults. The idea of one culture being superior to another reflects social conditioning and how behavior is affected by the belief.

When I was fifteen, I spent a month working on an archeological dig. I was talking to one of the archeologists one day during our lunch break and he asked those kinds of "getting to know you" questions you ask young people: Do you play sports? What is your favorite subject? And I told him, no I do not play any sports. I do theater, I am in choir, I play the violin and piano, I used to take art classes.

And he went WOW. That is amazing! And I said, "Oh no, but I'm not any good at ANY of them."

And he said something then that I will never forget, and which absolutely blew my mind because no one had ever said anything like it to me before: "I don't think being good at things is the point of doing them. I think you've got all these wonderful experiences with different skills, and that all teaches you things and makes you an interesting person, no matter how well you do them."

And that honestly changed my life. Because I went from a failure, someone who had not been talented enough at anything to excel, to someone who did things because I enjoyed them. I had been raised in such an achievement-oriented environment, so inundated with the myth of Talent, that I thought it was only worth doing things if you could "Win" at them. (Grissom, *Follies of God*)

A TROUBLESOME INHERITANCE
BY NICHOLAS WADE

As recently as 2014 a *New York Times* Bestseller, *A Troubelsome Inheritance* by Nicholas Wade tries to convince the reader that race can be explained by an evolutionary theory, but this theory is not based on science, but pseudo-science. He stated in his Preface that "[d]ifferences between populations undoubtedly exist but they are quite subtle. Far from being distinct, races differ merely in the quality known to geneticists as relative allele frequency." Harvard University paleogeneticist, David Reich, noted "[t]here are no fixed traits associated with specific geographic locations, because as often as isolation has created differences among populations, migration and mixing have blurred or erased them" (61).

Nicholas Wade's early background afforded him an excellent opportunity to acquire knowledge of the myth of European supremacy. He was born in Aylesbury, United Kingdom in 1942, educated at Eton College, and earned a Bachelor's degree in Natural Sciences in 1964, from King's College in Cambridge. He came to America in 1970 and worked as a writer and editor for various journals, focusing mostly on science and nature. He worked at *The New York Times* as a staff and editorial writer from 1982 until 2012. His stance in *A Troublesome Inheritance* comes as no surprise since he first gained notoriety for his favorable treatment of the controversial book, *Sociobiology: The New Synthesis* by E.O. Wilson. In reading Wade's book one can see the influence of Wilson's work.

Wade's primary mistake was in accepting race as the biological invention of a subspecies. He noted in defense of himself that "referring to anyone who explores the biological basis of race as a 'scientific racist,' and thus in essence demonizing them as racists, the academic left has managed to suppress almost all discussion of human differentiation." Wade failed to reference the statement of the American Anthropological Association that said in essence that the best available research shows race to be a social construct that is biologically invalid.

The organizations involved in the scientific studies of genetics dismissed the idea of races or subspecies as early as 1738 except for those who wanted to promote the myth of Anglo-Saxon superiority and domination over all other nations. Wade received negative criticism about his claim of biological races and stated that "I have seen no reason to modify the argument of [*A Troublesome Inheritance*] first half, that race has a biological basis, one that is founded in the subtle quality of relative allele frequency. Far from offering any basis for racism, this scientific fact only emphasizes the genetic unity of humankind."

Wade's use of the word race automatically dooms his work because race is not a scientific word and has no fixed meaning or definition. Greg Laden, a biological anthropologist, who did a detailed critical analysis of Wade's book, entitled "A Troubling Tome" echoed that sentiment. Regarding Wade's use of race Laden noted that "[w]ithout boundaries or predictive value, race isn't a valid biological concept. Human races may have existed in the past—just as there are subspecies of different mammals, including chimpanzees—and they could exist in the future. Nonetheless, to this point in the history of Homo sapiens has not led to a known emergence of distinct races." He added that "[w]e evolved recently, spread quickly, and in many regions interacted readily. Race is a powerful and important social construct, and in that way, it is very real, but it is not a biological useful concept for understanding human diversity." Regardless of the efforts of other scientists to debunk race as a scientific term, the word continues to have currency.

We were told by Laden that "Wade's book touched off a firestorm of controversy—as he surely knew it would. It is the latest in a series of dispatches concerning human variation, whose authors in recent decades have starkly divided into two camps one centered in anthropology and the other in psychology. Wade is in the latter camp." Consequently, the people that believe in the concept of race found Wade's book to be informative and as Charles Murray noted "a delight to read— conversational and lucid. And it will trigger an intellectual explosion the likes of which we haven't seen for a few decades" (*The Wall Street Journal*). People are accepting of information when science is associated with the subject and often do not question the findings unless something out of the ordinary catches their attention. However, if one already shares the ideas and opinions presented in the work, then no controversy exists. Again, we witness via Wade's work the promotion of the myth of Anglo- Saxon supremacy using the language of race.

Wade is in no way unaware of the fact that the information he promotes is part of pseudo-science regarding race. However, Wade continues to point a finger at scientists who recognize the dangers involved in the continued use of the word race and the protection it provides for the myth of European supremacy; and not at the term itself. He claims that those people are the problem, not race. He stated that "politically driven distortion of scientific views about race can be traced to a sustained campaign from the 1950s onward by the anthropologist Ashley Montagu who sought to make the word race taboo, at least when referring to people" (Wade 68-69). What appears like a character assassination, Wade describes

Montagu as a biased person "who was Jewish, grew up in the East End district of London, where he experienced considerable anti- Semitism." In other words, Montagu was not an Anglo-Saxon, Nordic, or real European that would support the myth.

Wade's reference to Montagu's effort beginning in the 1950s is incorrect, they began in the 1940s. Wade knew also that language and especially the use of the word race served as protection of the myth. After noting that Montagu studied in London and New York as an anthropologist under Franz Boas, who he referred to as the champion of racial equality and the belief human behavior is the direct result of culture, he noted that Montagu became passionate about the dangers of race and quoted Montagu's references to race. "Race is the witchcraft, the demonology of our time, the means by which we exorcise the imagined demonical powers among us…It is the contemporary myth, humankind's most dangerous myth, America's Original Sin" (69).

A *New York Times Book Review* article on August 8, 2014, was critical of Wade's book relative to its thesis "that argued that human evolution has been 'recent, copious, and regional' and that genes may have influenced a variety of behaviors that underpin differing form of human society." This thesis is Wade's way of trying to support the myth of European supremacy through biology. The article concluded that "[t]he book has been widely denounced by scientists, including many of those upon whose work the book was based."

CHAPTER 3

WORKS JUSTIFYING THE CONCEPT OF EUROPEAN SUPREMACY

We have seen where a mixture of science, history, and statistics can go a long way in convincing people that a myth is not a myth but indeed, the truth. Ignoring the fact that Linnaeus showed no biological differences among the variety of Homo sapiens, the bigots proceeded to use Darwin's book to try and convince others to accept the legitimacy of their myth. As one scholar noted that "[i]n the 19th century, Darwin's discoveries made an enormous impact in England, Western Europe, their colonies, and the USA, where

Christianity was the dominant religion." A conflict between Darwin's work and what the Bible said about creation and what the promoters of the myth of European supremacy wanted people to believe: Although "Darwin's theory was seen to be in conflict with the literal interpretation of special creation to be found in the Bible in the Book of Genesis, and even today Darwin's work raises emotional responses among fundamentalists" promoters of the myth of European Supremacy still wanted to utilize it for their purpose.

Religion was used as a weapon of Anglo-Saxon, European supremacy alongside science and statistics. However, it started shortly before then in print. One of the earliest printed and published selections was by Cotton Mather. The Puritans considered Mather to be royalty since he was named after both grandfathers who were leaders in the Puritan community. The question concerning the appropriateness of a Christian owning enslaved people and supporting slavery caused anxiety for the church. In his work, Mather attempts to allay the feelings of guilt experienced by the Christians by using the concepts of Christianity and biblical references to make his point.

Mather was the most prolific Puritan writer of his day, and indeed, wrote on practically any subject that was of interest to him. One of his faults was he frequently contradicted himself as he developed his discussions. The feelings and attitudes Anglo-Saxons and European Americans had relative to the enslaved Africans were negative and based primarily on their black skin color. In Europe, the color black was associated with the devil, evil, fear, and most things negative, so it was easy for the throng to be influenced into hating Africans because of their dark skin.

THE NEGRO CHRISTIANIZED
BY COTTON MATHER (1706)

Cotton Mather, a leader in the Puritan church, wrote this pamphlet to let his people know that owning enslaved people was okay for Christians if the Christians saved the souls of the enslaved. Consequently, the slaveholders would gain heavenly benefits by converting the souls of these heathens into pure God-fearing, master-obeying ones. Mather presented the proposition thusly: "That *for a man to know the Art of Alms, is more than for a man to be crowned with the Diadem of Kings: But to Convert one Soul unto God, is more than to pour out Ten Thousand Talents into the Baskets of the Poor*" (Lehman 121).

One of the ironies in reading and studying history is the influence that language played in the treatment of the conquered people. In fact, the language used by the conquers served to justify their treatment of the people conquered. For example, before the pilgrims and Puritans came to America, they identified the Indigenous people as savages and heathens. These labels were important because they justified the treatment of the Indigenous people by the pilgrims and Puritans from both a secular and religious perspective. However, ironically, the conquerors often behaved savagely towards their victims.

When we examine the language used by the Anglo-Saxons and early Americans relative to the enslaved Africans, the labels included savages, Negroes (to deny them actual identities), brutes, heathens, and barbarians, to list a few. Each of these labels somehow justified viewing the enslaved people as less than human beings and permitted them to be treated like property. When Cotton Mather wrote on the enslaved Africans, his focus was more on the enslavers rather than the enslaved. He employs the concepts of Christianity, God, Christ, and religion to build an argument for the enslavers to gain spiritual value and treasures by saving the souls of the enslaved. He stated, "*to Raise a Soul,* from a dark State of Ignorance and Wickedness to the knowledge of God, and the Belief of Christ, and the practice of our Holy and Lovely RELIGION; 'Tis the noblest Work, that ever was undertaken among the children of men" (121).

Consequently, the focus was on the anticipated benefits gained by the enslavers rather than any concern for the enslaved. As for the enslaved Africans, Mather's description of them underscores the level of contempt in which he held. He stated to the enslavers that "you may not be the Happy *Instruments,* of Converting, the *Blackest* Instances of *Blindness* and *Baseness,* into *admirable* Candidates of Eternal Blessedness. Let not this Opportunity be Lost; if you have any concern for *Souls,* your Own or Others" (121). From the description of the enslaved Africans one wonders if any hope exists for their salvation.

Mather does not argue about the wrongness or ills of slavery, instead, he focused on the selective quotes from the Bible to make his point that the enslaved people are not only seen as servants, but also as one's neighbors, and that they should be treated the way the enslavers want to be treated. He said "*God hath made of one Blood, all Nations of men,* he [the enslaved] is thy brother too" (123). Therefore, Mather viewed the enslaved as men or human beings, just not comparable to the Anglo- Saxons and Europeans.

Mather's essay takes his readers through a series of arguments all meant to benefit the Christian enslaver. After declaring that God gave the owners of the enslaved an opportunity to do the service of saving the souls of their enslaved, he goes on to present the responsibilities of the Christian enslavers. He questions the sincerity of the enslavers as Christians if they refuse to accept their responsibility of expanding the Christian family. "With what Face can you call yourselves *Christians?* If you do nothing that you[r] *Servants* also may become *Christian?*" He continued by explaining what the false Christian might expect: "What is he, who is willing that those of *his own House* remain Strangers to the *Faith,* and Wretched *Infidels?* Householder, Call thyself anything but a *Christian!*" (124). He admonishes the enslavers to make their servants Christians because the personal advantages outweigh the disadvantages from Mather's perspective as a Christian.

So, what rewards await the Christian enslaver that Christianizes his or her servants? Mather stated: "*Tho'my* Negroes *will not prove a part of the Israel of God, and will not be gathered unto the Lord, yet my work is with my God, and what I do is glorious in the Eyes of the Lord.*" For the Christian, Mather said that his kindness towards his servants is the greatest thing they can do.

Three significant things stand out in Mather's essay: one is that he identifies himself and the Anglo-Saxons, European Americans as Christians, then as white; second, he considered the enslaved people as human being based on his Christian beliefs; third, the tone of the essay suggests that Christianity belongs to the Anglo-Saxons and Europeans because they are the only ones blessed by God to own enslaved people.

The essay represents the Puritan church at this time in history when it recognized Mather as the church's leader. We, nevertheless, wonder about the status of those individuals that were not Christians but were owners of enslaved people. Mather used the phrase wretched infidel when referring to the non-Christian enslaver and as such would not be in the good graces of God. To convince the enslavers of their lack of support in using the color of the enslaved complexion as proof of their inferiority, Mather presented a convincing argument against the folly of such an argument. He mentioned that God would not go by a people's complexion to grant them favor. He then challenges the myth of white superiority based on color by saying that: "it is well known That the *Whites* are the least part of Mankind. The biggest part of Mankind, perhaps, are *Copper-Coloured* a sort of *Tawnies.*" To summarize the argument, Mather stated that "God who *looks on the Heart,* is not moved by the colour of the *skin;* is not more propitious to one *Color* than another" (133). The responsibility to save the souls of the enslaved people, as far as Mather was concerned, rested with the Anglo-Saxon, white, Christian people.

However, by 1782 the attitude towards the enslaved by their Christian owners had changed according to an account of an incident involving a clergyman and one of his parishioners. After a sermon by the clergyman where he appealed for more compassion for the enslaved that introduced the benignity of Christianity and the appeal for a greater degree of compassion for the enslaved, he was met with admonishment. One audience member said "we pay you a genteel salary to read to us the prayers of the liturgy, and to explain to us such parts of the Gospel as the rule of the church directs; but we do not want you to teach us what we are to do with our black"(Crevecoeur 657). No further admonishments were given by the clergyman.

Suffice it to say that the separation between the church and the holders of enslaved humans became more apparent each day. However, the use of religion and especially Christianity interpreted by individuals supportive of the European supremacy myth.

OUR COUNTRY
BY JOSIAH STRONG (1885)

Although the end of the Civil War made physical slavery illegal and African American a citizen, the attitudes and beliefs that viewed European Americans as superior to all people of color did not change; in fact, they expanded. The efforts to justify and validate European supremacy took on added weapons to garner trust, belief, and support for the false myth. We have already observed how science, nature, and history were used in these efforts, but in the 19th and 20th centuries introduced Christianity played a major role.

One of the leading voices in America for religious and social changes of the time was Josiah Strong (1847-1916). Strong believed that religion could resolve America's social and economic ills, not traditional religion, but revolutionary Christianity. This novel approach to religion came to be known as Christian Socialism. While the concept of this form of Christianity seemed rewarding for the nation, the rewards would only benefit Anglo-Saxons. His views and actions included people of color, but only in an inferior way since his objective was the expansion of Cotton Mather's idea of Christians saving the souls of the enslaved and protecting the myth of Anglo-Saxon and European supremacy. "In the 1890's he also emerged as one of the country's strongest voices in support of American imperialism, a philosophy that held that the nation needed to expand its sphere of influence around the world to ensure its continued primacy and save heathen cultures" (Encyclopedia).

Strong's initial notoriety was the result of reworking a manual used by the Congregational Missionary Society and publishing it as *Our Country*. The book contained aspects of his strongly held beliefs as well as assessments of social and economic problems facing America. Strong focused primarily on the overcrowded and poverty-ridden conditions caused by immigrants in the cities. Because he viewed himself as a Christian Anglo-Saxon and America belonging to Anglo-Saxons, it was their responsibility to protect and preserve their supremacy from the threat posed by inferior populations. As an expansionist, "Strong contended that the moral superiority of the nation's white population made America duty-bound to help 'lift up' the inferior members of other nations. The Anglo-Saxon race, he wrote, was "of unequaled energy, with all the majesty of numbers and the might of wealth behind it" (*Swift Papers*). Strong believed that because of the Anglo-Saxons' largest liberty, purest Christianity, and highest civilization, it was their duty to have influence over the world. Strong assumed that God had chosen them to represent humanity through Christianity. He also assumed that Christianity was made for the European (white) people. He expanded the term Anglo-Saxon to include European Americans that spoke English. The publication of his book *Our Country* vaulted Strong into the national limelight and led to his appointment as secretary of a Protestant ecumenical agency known as the American Evangelical Alliance. Following his success with his book *Our Country*, Strong published another book that had comparable success, *The New Era or, The Coming Kingdom*.

THE NEW ERA OR THE COMING KINGDOM
BY JOSIAH STRONG (1893)

In this new book Strong articulated ideas and philosophies that indicated a focus on his beliefs relative to his Christian Socialism and his full acceptance of the European supremacy myth. He believed that humanity could change for the better by paying attention to two areas. He noted that "progress of the race [Anglo-Saxon] in the future as in the past must be along these same two lines, the development of the individual and the organization of society" (31). He believed that God was directing his efforts to move the race forward and "methods of quickening the movement of the race along these two lines of progress, thus co-operating intelligently with the divine's plans, will be presented in later chapters." According to Strong, "[s]cience, which is a revelation of God's laws and methods, enables us to fall into his plans intentionally and to co-operate with him intelligently for the perfecting of mankind, thus hastening forward the coming of the kingdom" (30).

Strong believed that "[t]he reason that we are civilized, and the inhabitants of Central Africa savage is that our ancestors were civilized and their savage. Surely our ancestors did more for us by being what they were than they could have done for savage Africa by any means" (345). The responsibility given to the Anglo-Saxons by God, according to

Strong, was to bring to fruition God's Kingdom. The plan of attack was threefold: 1. The divine mission was to prepare the world for Christ's coming; 2. Reflect the divine's method of preparing nations to do the work; 3. Guide them to its completion. These actions would solidify the

Anglo-Saxon's place as the superior race: and therefore, of the utmost significance that of these characteristics, each of which single sufficed to make a nation supremely important in the world's history, all three unite in the one Anglo-Saxon race" (347).

Paul R. Griffin commented on these two works of Strong and described them as "the most vehement and most cunningly nuanced theological and scientific defense of white supremacy by any Christian leader of modern times" (*Seeds of Racism* 45). Griffin explained how Strong combined the two areas:

> To prove his point, he turned to both world history and Christian history, arguing that God in the beginning created three ancient races—the Hebrews, the Greeks, and the Romans. Exhibiting a robust affinity with Georg Wilhelm Hegel's theory of the dialectical development of human history, Strong asserted that God's sole purpose for these ancient races was that they evolve to a specific point, after which the Anglo-Saxons in Europe were to ascend to a still higher level. Coming still later—after the European race—the American Anglo-Saxons alone would evolve into the chosen people of God, who would finally usher in the long-awaited dominion of God on earth. (45-46)

With the combination of science and Christianity used as his tools, Strong was able to influence thousands of his followers into accepting his view of God's plan for the Anglo-Saxons. One result of his work was to strengthen the tribal concept among Anglo-Saxons and European Americans. Although Americans realized the fallacy of Strong's perception of ethnic supremacy, their efforts to debunk them were not enough to overcome the tribalism invented through his works. Throughout his works, Strong focused on Western history and Christianity as the sources of life and civilization for the world. When he wrote of non-western people or cultures, he usually prefaced his comments with descriptive adjectives such as heathen or barbaric to establish a negative and inferior mindset for the reader regarding those people and cultures.

We are reminded that the power of language was a method of control that the "[m]ost outspoken in this regard was Josiah Strong, who predicted in the 1880s that the world was about 'to enter upon a new stage of its history—the final competition of races for which the Anglo-Saxon is being schooled" (Jacobson 207). For Strong, God had placed on the Europeans or Anglo-Saxons the task of bringing his Kingdom into existence. And they would be the only ones to enjoy it.

Lest we forget, others in America during this time were also spreading their theories and opinions about the superiority of the socalled white Americans. Strong, however, chose to focus on the Anglo-Saxons in America as God's select group to bring in the kingdom.

CHRISTIANITY AND THE SOCIAL CRISIS
BY WALTER RAUSCHENBUSCH (1907)

If the reader of Strong and Rauschenbusch's books were to look for a direct reference to the status of African Americans in society, he would be hard-pressed to do so because their ideas and opinions relative to people of color reside in comments concerning evolution. In other words, the assumptions of both Strong and Rauschenbusch following Darwin's work on evolution is that the Africans or people of color did not evolve beyond the level of brutes and barbarians. That being the case, they could not have made any significant contribution to the development of humankind. So, to consider people of color as inclusive in the building of American society and the world is not likely; they were counterproductive to the growth of civilization.

An example offered in support of his concept of African Americans being inferior to Anglo-Saxons and European Americans, Rauschenbusch discussed why the south lost the Civil War. He believed the "reason why the South broke down in our Civil War was that its slave labor had kept it industrially incompetent" (Griffin 47). His statement, while meant to disparage the enslaved African Americans, indicates the lack of diligence of the slave masters. The fact that the enslaved people were seen as lacking in productivity regarding their labor speaks to the hypocrisy and lies of a country that enriched the South, America, Europe, and the world through their blood, sweat, and tears.

Being familiar with scientific theories of his day as well as being an evangelical Christian theologian, Rauschenbusch was able to develop his own theories about the coming of the king and his kingdom. His ethnic bigotry convinced him to show in his work an acceptance of the African American as a creation of God, but different from the Anglo-Saxons and would not be suitable for participation in the coming Kingdom of God. Griffin noted that Rauschenbusch shared similar beliefs of many like-minded men of his age and "that both religion and science confirmed that 'the negro is a different being from the white man, and therefore, of necessary, was designed by the Almighty Creator to live a different life" (49).

As these publications indicate, being white, Anglo-Saxon, European, and European American did not carry the same value; being white was the prize. The primary objective of these publications was to try and validate the myth of European supremacy by almost any means necessary. The myth of European supremacy was part of the normal mindset of Americans, although they knew it to be false, they assumed a life where they viewed make-believe as reality, and reality as make-believe.

American society began with the mindset of Anglo-Saxon superiority primarily for European males and built their system of government with that myth at the center. The language from the Declaration of Independence to the U.S. Constitution focused on the lives and well-being of the European male's power and control of society. We see this philosophy underscored in the works of Stone and others who make no apology for invoking their interpretation of the Bible and placing the Anglo-Saxon, European male at the top of the social letter. They promote the Bible as the supreme authority for guiding their lives and that of America. Because they use the Bible as a given element of trust, they received little if any criticism or challenges. Therefore, the people in their audiences need no additional prompt to accept the view of America as a land created by God for the Anglo-Saxon European males to dominate and control.

CHAPTER 4
THE ART OF DISBELIEF

Movies are one of the most popular forms of entertainment in the world. The genre does not matter as long as it is entertaining. Our emotions can and often do run the gambit of interest from mystery, romance, drama, comedy, suspense, and others. We become engulfed in the action and simply enjoy the experience. The one thing that allows us to have these experiences is our ability to step away from reality. In other words, we must have a willing suspension of disbelief to fully enjoy the movie knowing full well that what we are witnessing is not real.

For many years, America has lived with a willing suspension of disbelief relative to ethnic bigotry and European supremacy. When the murder of George Floyd was broadcast to the world on television, protests erupted throughout the world. Why? Society conditioned Americans to think of ethnic bigotry as an American phenomenon. So why did other parts of the world protest? Was it in support of the marginalized

Americans, empathy for the death of a human being, or was it for another reason?

The truth is that ethnic bigotry is global and in the form of European Supremacy and dominance. While socially conditioned Americans look at skin color and think in terms of race as the center of bigotry, the fact is that ethnicity is the real focus and center of the bias; that is, according to the myth, Europeans occupy the top position as superior and dominant in relation to all other human beings.

Hypocrisy exists in that the powers that control society promote one system of political and moral beliefs while they practice another system that is the opposite. The two systems exist in parallel forms one human and one non-human. The myth maintains that the human is viewed and treated better than the non-human because belief in the myth of European superiority and domination allowed the Europeans to define who are humans and who are non-humans, as well as what is considered normal or not normal based on whatever they select as the deciding factor—skin color, religion, culture, geography, intelligence, etc.

While Europeans know and act out the myth of supremacy, they constantly deny its existence. However, in 1969 an article in *Foreign Affairs*, reported that the world "was still by and large a Western White-dominated world. The long-established assumptions and mythologies about race and color were still mostly taken for granted....[W]hite supremacy was a generally assumed and accepted state of affairs in the United States as well as in Europe's empires" (27). Mills added that "statements of such frankness are rare or nonexistent in mainstream white opinion today, which generally seeks to rewrite the past so as to deny or minimize the obvious fact of global white domination."

Gary Younge, a professor of Sociology at the University of Manchester commented on the protest ignited by the murder of George Floyd: "Some of the biggest demonstrations were in Paris. Many European leaders at the time dismissed the notion that the protest had any domestic relevance." Their doubt suggested a fear of the truth being revealed. Younge continued with "the French were more insistent than most, claiming that 'white privilege' and 'intersectionality' were American concepts imported to sow division and rancor" (18). Admitting to white privilege would suggest an acknowledgment of the myth and its social acceptance.

The focus of an article called "Europe's War on Woke" by James McAuley, a Paris-based writer, was the desire of Europeans and European Americans to defend the efforts to unveil the delusions of European supremacy. McAuley introduced the terms "woke", "cancel culture", and "cultural imperialism" to explain why the "elites across the Atlantic are freaking out about the concept of structural racism." The terms "woke" and "cancel culture" used in America "has to do with the push for racial equality and against systemic racism." However, " what is labeled 'woke' is often whatever social movement a particular country's establishment fears most" (*The Nation* 20). Movements, therefore, can be discredited by changing the significance of the terms. The term woke is viewed as belonging to America and in so doing to refer to them as American is to say they don't apply to Europe.

In the mid-fifties, I attended a parochial high school where I was the only African American student. The concept of having a willing suspension of disbelief by my European American classmates and teachers always represented a challenge to me. My being active in sports, debate, and choir presented other experiences that caused me to wonder about my classmates and teachers. For example, whenever I traveled with the school's choir or sports teams, the school made frequent convenient stops for food and drinks. I had three choices: stay on the bus, get off the bus and walk around it, or try and get service from the rear of the establishment where we stopped. Classmates and teachers knew that the business owners discriminated against me and treated me as a non-person as well as I. Nevertheless, no one ever said a word in protest because they knew that was the norm.

The challenge for me was whenever the choir or the teams recited the Pledge of Allegiance, or a creed or quote that underscored fairness and justice for all, I wondered just how they pictured me and themselves, if they thought about it at all. During those times, my behavior was non-threatening, but my feelings were alert to the hypocrisy and bigotry best depicted in the poem by Paul Laurence Dunbar "We Wear the Mask."

> We wear the mask that grins and lies,
> It hides our cheeks and shades our eyes,
> This debt we pay to human guile;
> With torn and bleeding hearts we smile,
> And mouth with myriad subtleties.
> Why should the world be otherwise,
> In counting all our tears and sighs?
> Nay, let them only see us, while
> We wear the mask.
> We smile, but O great Christ, our cries
> To thee from tortured souls arise.
> We sing, but oh the clay is vile
> Beneath our feet, and long the mile;

But let the world dream otherwise,

We wear the mask!

The mask was a form of self-protection both mentally and physically from the deceptions witnessed daily. What occurs in America constantly is this process of reversal, like what prisoners experience when they enter prison for a long time; they must adjust to a whole new world inside the prison because not adjusting could be a life-or-death experience. Mills described what happens in America based on an atmosphere of ethnic bigotry: "Racism, racial self-identification, and race thinking are then not in the least 'surprising,' 'anomalous,' 'puzzling,' incongruent with Enlightenment European humanism, but *required* by the Racial Contract [belief in and acceptance of the myth of European Supremacy] as part of the terms for the European appropriation of the world." The phrase "European Supremacy" serves the purpose of expressing the concept of a Racial Contract. Mills continued by saying "standard contractarian discussions are fundamentally misleading because they have things backward to begin with: what has usually been taken (when it has been noticed at all) as the racist '*exception*' has really been the *rule*; what has been taken as the 'rule,' the ideal norm, has really been the exception" (122).

What has happened historically is that European scientists, scholars, clergy, and others that have accepted the myth of European Supremacy develop theories and approaches to perpetuate, protect, and promote the concept. For example, when Morton began collecting skulls and labeling them based on his concept of race, which we know is not dependable because Morton never defined it, but scientists and scholars applauded his efforts. Of course, the European skull was used by Morton as the model of normality. While this was a case of the blind leading the blind, the ploy has worked for Europeans for years.

A willing suspension of disbelief for European Americans happens daily. Their experience is comparable to them visiting Disneyland. People going to Disneyland know they are going to a make-believe place for entertainment. Once inside Disneyland, they subsequently leave the real world behind and accept Disneyland as their reality. While experiencing life in Disneyland visitors have little to remind them of the real world outside except time and money; that is, they know that Disneyland will close at a certain time and that they must continue to spend money with cash or credit cards to enjoy themselves. However, once outside Disneyland, a degree of reality returns to the European Americans, but a large degree of that willing suspension of disbelief remains in the form of how they view themselves as privileged European Americans because of their skin color. They know that their skin color has value in a make-believe society that ignores the truth of the false concept of race. They also know that time is quickly running out on the myth because of society's changing demographics. While a segment of Americans will understand and accept this necessary transition from make-believe to reality, others will not willingly make the change.

For over two hundred years, Americans have witnessed and experienced the effects of ethnic bigotry on themselves and others. What the victims of this bigotry have viewed and experienced from European Americans have been their acceptance of a willful suspension of disbelief regarding race and its language knowing that the concept was false and damaging but choosing to ignore it and to remain silent about its effects on its victims.

The behavior of European Americans living with a suspension of disbelief was the subject of a study and subsequently a book entitled *White Fragility* by Dr. Robin DiAngelo. What dictates this behavior and clearly underscores the suspension of disbelief she identifies as a fixed system of conditioning:

> This systemic and institutional control allows those of us who are white in North America to live in a social environment that protects and insulates us from race-based stress. We have organized society to reproduce and reinforce our racial interests and perspectives. Further, we are centered in all matters deemed normal, universal, benign, neutral, and good.

DiAngelo, by identifying herself as part of this group, earns her credibility with references to the experiences she discusses. She further explains the behavior and why the suspension of belief works well for the Europeans:

> Socialized into a deeply internalized sense of superiority and entitlement that we are either not consciously aware of or can never admit to ourselves, we become highly fragile in conversations about race…Thus, we perceive any attempt to connect us to the system of racism as a very unsettling and unfair moral offense.

In addition, DiAngelo describes how European Americans behave when someone challenges their biased ethnic psyche: "White Fragility is a state in which even a minimum amount of racial stress becomes intolerable, triggering a range of defensive moves. These moves include the outward display of emotions such as anger, fear, and guilt, and behaviors such as argumentation, silence, and leaving the stress-inducing situation." To make certain the reader understood the phenomena of white fragility stress, DiAngelo presented a variety of examples in the form of statements:

1. Suggesting that a white person's viewpoint comes from a racialized frame of reference

2. People of color choosing not to protect the racial feelings of white people regarding race

3. Being present with a person of color in a position of leadership

On one occasion I experienced these three white fragilities in action; they occurred after I had just completed a lecture for a state humanities program on the novel *The Monster* by Walter Dean Myers. The novel is about a fifteen-year-old African American teenager accused of committing murder, a charge for which we presume he is innocent. He lived in a low socio-economic African American community and was represented in court by a Public Defender. The challenge he faced was not unusual for African Americans: his lawyer, the prosecutor, the judge, and the jury were all European Americans. The first challenge his lawyer expressed to him was that she must convince the jury that he was a human being and not a monster.

During the lecture, I pointed out that similar themes existed in the novels, *A Lesson Before Dying* by Earnest Gaines and *To Kill a Mockingbird* by Harper Lee, where in all three works an African American male faced death at the hand of a European American judge and jury. In all three novels, society viewed African American males as animals rather than human beings. All three lawyers in the novels faced the same problem of ethnic bigotry relative to the jury. The point made in the lecture was to show that ethnic bias against African American males was not something new, but was instead, ordinary in the American society represented in the works.

A question-and-answer session followed the lecture and one participant asked if ethnic bigotry existed in society. My response was that it was a fabric of society given our history and had been for years prior to the Civil War.

The director of the program took offense to my statement concerning ethnic bigotry and expressed doubt about European Americans being bigots. She stated forcefully that she was not a bigot, showing the stress from the first sign of white fragility mentioned above. I explained to her that this theme of bigotry was present in all the novels and that avoiding it during the discussion would prove difficult.

She followed her argument by asking me not to refer to European Americans as bigots because they were not and would feel hurt when labeled as such, showing stress as indicated in the second statement of DiAngelo's.

I told her that I was simply presenting information relative to the novel *Monster,* to help the readers understand important aspects of the story. She said that she believed emphasizing that bigotry was part of American society was not an acceptable feature for the lecture and she considered it inappropriate. We parted ways when I told her that my responsibility in analyzing and discussing literature was to focus on what the literature provided, not how I might feel about the content. She continued to disagree about the feelings of the audience. Her comments reflected the sentiment of the third statement regarding White Fragility.

The white fragility phenomenon describes the behavior of people living the mindset of a suspension of disbelief. Stress occurs when the possibility of reality threatens to break through to reveal the falseness of the perception. In other words, DiAngelo's book describes how European Americans act while experiencing the benefits of so-called "White Privilege".

The subtitle of the book *White Fragility: Why it's so hard for white people to talk about racism,* points to the challenge facing European Americans: In order to talk about racism, European Americans have to confront the delusion of living in a make-believe world where they enjoy power and privileges. DiAngelo stated that "White fragility is much more than mere defensiveness or whining. It may be conceptualized as the *Sociology of dominance*: an outcome of white people's socialization into white supremacy and a means to protect, maintain, and reproduce white supremacy" (113).

DiAngelo underscored European supremacy in her statement that "white people raised in Western society are conditioned into a white supremacist worldview because it is the bedrock of our society and its institutions" (129). For European Americans to talk about race would open the door to an examination of the myth of European supremacy they want to protect. We can readily witness that reaction from the various calls by European Americans to not teach Critical Race Theory (CRT) to their children.

The reactions by segments of European Americans to CRT are a prime example of white fragility and the use of language to invent social chaos based on bigotry. What began as a discussion on race issues in a class taught by Dr. Derrick Bell in 1990 to university law students at Harvard has turned into a mysterious educational phenomenon that threatens the happiness and self-value of all European American children. The concern of European American parents and others for the damage this CRT can do to children is so great that eight states have written and passed laws prohibiting the teaching in which "any individual should feel discomfort, guilt, anguish or any other form of psychological distress on account of his or her race or sex" (Williams 15).

To add insult to injury, we know that teaching critical race theory is not acceptable in any K-12 schools, but usually only in college and university classes. The very people that are in arms about its teaching have no idea of its substance because the theory is neither defined nor fixed in its meaning. Nonetheless, eight states thought the matter serious enough to write and pass laws against teaching it in their schools. The mere mention of the phrase CRT is enough to cause concern for those European Americans that believe their children's feelings might be hurt by hearing anything about race or sex. Unfortunately, that concern is not by coincidence, but the deliberate product of an individual.

The use and manipulation of language has long been a tool of certain individuals that want to mislead and confuse people to control them and their behavior; Christopher Rufo is such an individual. His professional background included working as a senior analyst at the Manhattan Institute along with working as a Trump political organization. Rufo said that his objective "was to 'run a public persuasion campaign' that would conflate any number of topics and deposit them into a new bucket called critical race theory." He continued by saying "[w]e have successfully frozen their brand— 'critical race theory'—into the public conversation and are steadily driving up negative perceptions" (17). The limits to which certain people will go to prohibit the truth from the public and to protect the European supremacy myth have no boundaries.

"The goal is to have the public read something crazy in the newspaper and immediately think 'critical race theory.' We have decodified the term and will recodify it to annex the entire range of cultural constructions that are unpopular with Americans." Rufo suggests that anything that challenges the myth of European supremacy will be unpopular with most Americans. The illusion must remain in place because reality is too uncomfortable for certain European Americans to experience.

What Rufo has successfully accomplished is to have the phrase" critical race theory" is code for anything viewed as anti-European American and unacceptable to them. The manipulation of the language by Rufo has resulted in a failed opportunity to gain experience and become enlightened. "This is what critical race theory has become: an effigy. It is whatever the world-creating power of Tucker Carlson and the Conservative Political Action Committee and QAnon say it is. It is a million Willie Hortons dressed up as teachers hired to feast on the brains of kindergartners, killing their innocence" (Williams 17). The primary objective, however, is the protection and promotion of the European supremacy myth, and what better way to achieve that objective than to invent fearful, threatening, and frightening false information that hides the truth and reality from the make-believe view of the European American world.

We witness the protection of European supremacy in the fights throughout America and Europe where the focus is "on opposing and attempting to refute allegations of 'institutional' or 'structural' racism." Europe sees itself as different from America in the sense that race is not an issue. France does not use terms like black and white in talking about its citizens and so it differs from America which has a history of identifying people as black and white. The interesting point behind these differences between the European countries and America is not to engage in discussions about race and racism, "[r]ather, the charge is typically meant to stifle the discussion altogether—even when that discussion is being led by European citizens describing their own lived experience" (23).

Society conditioned Americans in general and European Americans specifically to live lives of suspended reality. Coming to grips with reality is the challenge facing them in an ever-changing world. The challenge in facing reality encompasses expansions of the European supremacy mythology." Although it has been known for at least 70 years that race is undeniably a social construct and that those 18th-century thinkers were misguided in their assumptions, many scientists still labor under the belief that race is biologically real" (Saini 16).

CHAPTER 5

THE POWER OF CONTROL

When we survey all the various publications that promoted the European supremacy myth, we also notice that the most essential element derived from those publications is the belief in the myth. The fact that language is employed to promote the myth comes as no surprise, however, the fact that the language included elements that engender trust provided a reasonable understanding of certainty that the myth would continue to exist. Myths have two natural enemies—facts and truth. The appearance of either facts or truth regarding the myth will serve to debunk it unless the myth is so deeply embedded in the minds of the hearers that they accept no reasonable or logical information regarding its veracity. On the contrary, opponents' defenses will invent justification to guard against attempts to debunk the myth. Because the myth of European supremacy affords its adherents the sense of privilege and power over other people, it must be defended if it is to be retained. The history of this myth shows that the strength of its longevity comes from the control it maintains over people. The belief of the Europeans in the supremacy offered by the myth was not sufficient to satisfy them; they had to prove to the world that they were, indeed, supreme.

Spain was the first European country to show its prowess by going west and enslaving the people with whom it came into contact. The rationale for enslaving them was expressed by King George who wrote: "The pretext used by the Spaniards for enslaving the New World were extremely curious,' 'the propagation of the Christian religion was the first reason, the next was the [Indigenous] Americans differing from them in colour, manner and customs, all of which are too absurd to take the trouble of refuting'" (Roberts 24). The power to justify enslaving people as demonstrated by the Spaniards was simply to say they were not Christians and did not look European. King George understood that the myth of European supremacy was beginning to express itself through colonization and enslaving of people of color. His comments relative to this practice were "for the European practice of enslaving Africans…the very reasons urged for it will be perhaps sufficient to make us hold such practice in execration" (24). Whether or not the practice was loathing, it nevertheless continued.

Charles Mills in his book *The Racial Contract* acknowledged that rather than talk about European supremacy, European Americans prefer to leave things as they were which meant that "[t]he modern world was thusly expressly created as a *racially hierarchical* polity, globally dominated by Europeans." The normal and accepted understanding of power and control "was still by and large a Western, white-dominated world." Any arguments focusing on assumptions and beliefs about race and skin color were ignored because "[w]hite supremacy was a generally assumed and accepted state of affairs in the United States as well as in Europe's empires" (27). The primary course taken by the European countries to demonstrate their power and dominance and served to lift all of Europe was colonialism.

The fact remains that whether a colonizing country benefited directly from the country it dominated, other European countries within the European orbit did benefit. "There was a sense in which all Europeans shared in a heightened sense of power engendered by the success of any of them, as well as in the pool of material wealth...that the colonies produced" (Mills 35). Regarding Mills's position on European supremacy, Edward Johnson stated that "Mills understands racism in terms of white subordination of nonwhites, thereby collapsing many forms of oppression into the 'global white supremacy' on which he chooses to focus. "There is an opposition of us against them with multiple overlapping dimensions: Europeans versus non-Europeans (geography), civilized versus wild/ savage barbarians (culture), and Christian versus heathens (religion). But they all eventually coalesced into the basic opposition of white versus non-white." The efforts to protect and promote the belief in the Supremacy myth is always the primary interest of the Europeans according to Mills. The fact remains as well that these efforts to protect the myth are also efforts to withhold the truth.

As Younge reported, in France a political and intellectual society of elites exists as "a closed society—it is very homogenous—and who are not well-informed about the reality of society." These people do not mingle with people of diverse backgrounds and so no diversity exists among them. That being the case, we learn that "France is not the white man—there is a false vision[among] our elites about what France is—but they are afraid of this diversity. They see it as a threat to their reality."

The fear of their reality is a shared one with all those that embrace the European Supremacy myth because of the loss of control that comes with that reality.

In her work, *White Fragility*, DiAngelo described the kind of society in which she lives and enjoys elements of power and control. "I am a white American raised in the United States. I have a white frame of reference and a white worldview, and I move through the world with a white experience. My experience is not a universal experience." She acknowledged that she sees herself through the eyes of a person living in the myth of European supremacy. The fear of having that self-image taken away and having to face reality is a continuous job of denial.

Life in a society that controls the denial of reality represents a challenge for European Americans, so one way to avoid having to deal with reality is to not acknowledge it. DiAngelo noted that: "Given how seldom we experience racial discomfort in a society we dominate, we haven't had to build our racial stamina. Socialized into a deeply internalized sense of superiority that we either are unaware of or can never admit to ourselves we become highly fragile in conversations about race." That fragility is an indication of fear of having to face reality. Continuing, she underscored the need for control: "We consider a challenge to our racial world views as a challenge to our very identities as good and moral people. Thus, we perceive any attempt to connect us to the system of racism as an unsettling and unfair moral offense." She identifies a variety of tactics employed by European Americans in an effort not to face reality or lose the power to control.

A brief example of how the power of control can work. My city has a fair-housing committee that usually meets one Thursday each month. I was asked to join the committee and did. During an early meeting, a mature European American and I started a conversation concerning our committee objectives. After the meeting, she invited me to lunch so that we might continue our discussion. I accepted and met with her at a local restaurant. Towards the end of our lunch, our waiter came with the ticket and before I could react, she took the ticket and said lunch was on her. I thanked her and we parted. For two more committee meetings, my new friend and I went to lunch after our meeting. Finally, after our fourth committee meeting, we agreed to meet again for lunch. This time, however, I arrived at the restaurant a little before her and asked the waiter to bring the check for the meal to me.

During lunch we had a good discussion about the things addressed by our committee. After our meal, the waiter brought the ticket to me. She tried to get the ticket from me, but I mentioned that she had paid for the past lunches, and I thought I would pay this time. Unfortunately, that was the last time she invited me to lunch or accepted my invitation to lunch. The adage about no free lunch applies here as well as the need for control. Because the power of control that came with paying for the meal was no longer available to her, she refused to no longer participate. We were always cordial towards each other at our meetings, but never again went to lunch together.

The reaction of my committee member is not out of the ordinary, Danielle Sered, a European American female, stated that "[w]hite people control people. We want people to behave a certain way and we use power to try to ensure that they do so." In addition, she noted how "[i]n our own [European American] families, relationships, and communities, we police behavior we regard as aberrant, as embarrassing, as strange, as improper, as rebellious, as imperfect, as somehow inconsistent with our superiority, and we try to stop that behavior" (*Until We Reckon* 219). Control is necessary to maintain a sense of balance in the fantasy world.

Although Sered's primary focus in her work is on mass incarceration, she sees the success of the criminal justice system based on control that functions in four ways: "control, (in the form of policing, punishment (in the forms ranging from fines to imprisonment), exile (in form of incarceration, and extermination (in the form of executions). But this way of being is also a recipe for violence. It assumes that behavior is shaped by power and control rather than connection and responsibility" (220). The quantity of recent protests by citizens in America and people across the globe is an indication that violence is the preferred way for authorities to control community relations. The behavior and desire for power to control society by European Americans speak to a certain mindset or psyche. An article, "The Psychology of Racism" by Peter Loewenberg, *The Great Fear,* Holt, Rinehart and Winston, Inc. 1970, discussed the behavior of European Americans (whites) pointing out how they acquire their ethnic prejudice.

Loewenberg writes that a socially conditioned European American child is directed by his everyday living environment and values present in that environment to acquire ethnic biases. Teaching him about ethnic bigotry and ethnic inferiority is not necessary because his observation and participation in his world inform him. Therefore, what the community presents as patterns of social behavior he accepts and conforms to which includes viewing people of color as inferior. "Even if he is intellectually convinced of their equality, it is difficult for him to escape the emotional consequences of his upbringing." Because of this social conditioning, his behavior will not differ from his environment.

The article stated that because of the social conditioning received in his environment, when the child encounters a person of color, the fixed stereotyped images of the person of color often serve to reinforce the support and confirm the stereotypes of the person of color. "The social stereotype of the Negro as lazy, amoral, dirty, and dangerous, bears an inertia that is doubly hard to break, for his low status is sustained by the majority white image, which in turn keeps the Negro in a depressed social and economic position and induces impulse-gratifying and aggressive behavior" (188). In other words, the person of color only has to be present for the European American to become uncomfortable and possibly aggressive towards him.

The subject of European American fear is also a focus of this article and Loewenberg identifies it as projection. "When forbidden desires emerge in a white man, he can facilitate their repression by projecting them onto blacks or members of other racial minorities. In the unconscious of the bigot the black represents his own repressed instincts which he fears and hates and which are forbidden by his conscience...." The struggle comes from his trying to conform to the professed values of his society.

He explained the process of projection:

This is why the black man becomes the personification of sexuality, Lewdness, laziness, dirtiness, and unbridled hostility. He is the symbol Of voluptuousness and the immediate gratification of pleasure. In the Deepest recesses of the minds of white Americans, Negroes are associated With lowly and debased objects or with sexuality and violence. In our society Children are taught at an early age that their excrement is disgusting, smelly, And dirty, and that sexual and hostile feelings are bad and dangerous. These Feelings are easily associated with low status or tabooed groups such as Negroes. Blacks are pictured in the unconscious imagery of the white majority as dark and odorous, aggressive, libidinal, and threatening. (192)

Loewenberg's article was published in 1970 and much has changed in America relative to the changing demographics as well as social improvements regarding ethnic groups. His remedy for ethnic bigotry was integration and education, especially for the young. Unfortunately, the element of ethnic bigotry and the challenge to protect and promote the myth of European supremacy has gained support despite overwhelming evidence debunking the myth.

When fear in an individual is present, it is usually joined by a particular mindset and related behavior; that is, the mind recognizes a challenge or threat to the safety and well-being of the person and the behavior exhibits a defense to calm the fear or eliminate it. However, if the basis of the fear is an avoidance of truth and reality, then the fear will be constant and so must be the defense—to prevent the truth or reality from manifesting itself. The term used by psychologists to describe this condition is cognitive dissonance. Most dictionaries view it as the state of having conflicting thoughts, beliefs, or attitudes, especially as relating to behavioral decisions and attitude changes, or "psychological conflict resulting from incongruous beliefs and attitudes held simultaneously" ("cognitive dissonance").

Cognitive dissonance is when "people hold a core belief that is very strong. When they are presented with evidence that works against that belief, the new evidence cannot be accepted. It would create a feeling uncomfortable, called cognitive dissonance. And because it is so important to protect the core belief, they will rationalize, ignore and even deny anything that doesn't fit in with the core belief" (Fanon qtd. on *Cram*).

Europeans as well as European Americans exhibited this condition well before slavery in America. However, the course of action used in protecting and promoting the myth of supremacy has taken various avenues and practices. Examining the elements of fear that suggest an acknowledgment of the threat or challenge to the reality that results in a loss of power and control is in order.

Currently, the primary tacit used to allay the fears of European Americans is an attack on education that presents the facts of American history unfiltered through a biased lens. That history shows how the European and European Americans built a society based on hypocrisy and brutal force justified by the belief in a myth of European supremacy. History shows the lengths to which a people will go to protect and promote the myth and defend against any effort for the revelation of the truth. The focus of the defense effort, captured in the phrase Critical Race Theory (CRT), is a college and university level program that looks at the factors related to the significance of race in America. The opponents of CRT claim that the teaching of this subject matter will be harmful to young children making them uncomfortable.

An NBC reporter characterized the problem by pointing out that those "condemning critical race theory haven't read it or studied it intensely. This is largely predicated on fear: the fear of losing power and influence and privilege," he said. "The larger issue that this is all stemming from is a desire to deny the truth about America, about racism." The fear of the CRT opponents is so great that twenty-two states have made and signed into law legislation prohibiting its teaching. The language of these laws leaves much to be desired relative to their interpretation.

The NBC reporter identified five states that have passed legislation: Idaho, Iowa, Oklahoma, Texas, and Tennessee. The reasons given for the laws vary with each state. "Legislators behind the Idaho bill said critical race theory 'tries to make kids feel bad.'" Lawmakers in Tennessee "said teaching about racism promotes 'division,' and a pending bill in Rhode Island bans teaching the idea that 'the United States of America is fundamentally racist or sexist.'" The action of the CRT opponents and their "fight over race and equity in schools is a coordinated one, backed by well-connected conservative groups and media outlets." The five states that have passed laws aimed at preventing the teaching of CRT all show a fear of the truth

Governor Brad Little of Idaho signed into law a bill whose focus is to restrict the teaching of CRT in state schools and universities. According to the May 6, 2021, report, "The bill, H 377, prevents teachers from "indoctrinating" students into belief systems that claim that members of any race, sex, religion, ethnicity or national origin are inferior or superior to other groups" *(The Guardian)*.

In Iowa, Governor Kim Reynolds signed into law a bill that restricts the teaching of CRT along with diversity training offered by the government as part of the classroom curriculum. In a statement reported by Brandon Richard, the Governor stated that "Critical Race Theory is about labels and stereotypes, not education. It teaches kids that we should judge others based on race, gender or sexual identity, rather than the content of someone's character."

Oklahoma's Governor, Kevin Stitt, signed HB 1775 that prohibits teaching where anyone "is "inherently racist, sexist or oppressive, whether consciously or unconsciously or that they should feel "discomfort, guilt, anguish or any other form of psychological distress' because of their race or sex." In addition, this law, "[u]nder rules imposedby the state, teachers or administrators found in violation of the law can lose their licenses, and schools can lose accreditation" (and Hylton).

The basic guidelines of the Tennessee law include a section that identifies concepts not to be taught. All fourteen of these statements include the terms race and sex, yet nowhere in the eleven pages of the guidelines are those terms defined. In addition, the laws allow politicians to dictate what educators can and cannot teach, which is a denial of their First Amendment rights.

Greg Abbott, Texas governor, signed a "controversial bill that prescribes how Texas teachers can talk about current events and America's history of racism in the classroom." The law "prohibits teaching certain concepts about race; develops a civics training program for teachers; and largely bars schools from giving credit to students for advocacy work." The law "also urges educators to teach only that slavery and racism are 'deviations' from the founding principles of the United States" (*Dallas News*).

Tennessee Governor Bill Lee sees CRT as divisive and un-American. He noted that "[i]t fundamentally puts groups of people above the sanctity of the individual which is a founding principle of this nation. It's appropriate that we would not teach critical race theory in this state" (*Action News*).

The ACLU stated on NBS News that the CRT "states that racism is embedded both in US history and modern American law. It holds that legal institutions in the US are inherently racist." Because the essence of that statement speaks truth, it must be challenged and denied by the opponents of CRT. When we look at the laws written against the teaching of CRT, we must wonder why they fear the truth. The simple answer is that the truth will show the hypocrisy Americans have lived with since before slavery.

CHAPTER 6

CORRECTING THE PROBLEM OF DISBELIEF

I f the problem facing America was simply cognitive dissonance, the avenue of approach to addressing it would be basics: identifying, assessing, and resolving the conflict. However, the primary problem facing America relative to its mindset is the fear of losing the power and control that comes with the truth of the European supremacy myth. As a means of protecting and denying the fact regarding the myth, supporters of the myth use words and phrases to avoid the actual problem—belief in the myth. Rather than focus on the myth, distractions are employed in words like race, racism, racist, racial, antiracism, diversity, and others as the source of America's ethnic bias problems. So, for example, if someone focuses on the problem of antiracism, nothing constructive can happen because the actual issue of acknowledging the European myth has not occurred.

The article "The Missing Story" by Kali Holloway examined the impact the media has on the fear problem. "We are deep in the throes of a white grievance movement, inflamed by fears that white dominance is decreasing. The media's coddling of white folks isn't helping." The media can be a positive influence on society if they would focus more attention on the cause of the fear rather than the fear. "As long as the story continues to privilege white fearmongering, the press should be considered a contributor to the problem of white supremacy in education." Too often take for granted that people working in the media are objective and bias-free; to believe that would be an enormous mistake.

Extensive books and articles written by scholars and others today focus on the term "antiracism" to educate and inform readers about what it is and how to overcome it. One problem with this endeavor is that first, one cannot overcome or eliminate a concept while constantly legitimizing it by using the term. Next, antiracism comes from racism which comes from race, a term invented to try and validate a false concept. Therefore, if the false concept of European supremacy is proven at the beginning, then all efforts relative to correcting antiracism are invalid. Einstein stated regarding problem solving that "no problem can be solved from the same level of consciousness that created it."

The governors of the states that signed into law prohibiting teaching about race, sex, gender, and diversity should know that these laws serve to give acceptability to the concept of race. Whenever the word race is employed, especially in laws, the myth of European supremacy is safe. The invented word race protects itself and the myth. If the writers and scholars that focus on race and its derivatives continue to do so, it means that they do not realize they are playing the language game.

Whether we realize it, we use language to say things we do not mean but think that it means what we want it to mean. For example, when someone sees an acquaintance who has a cold or sinus problem, we usually inquire as to their health. "What are you doing for that problem?" The acquaintance usually responds by telling how the problem is being addressed. Unfortunately, the acquaintance does not answer the question first posed. The correct answer should have been "nothing" because one would not want to encourage the malady to worsen by doing something for it. The intent of the first question was to ask what the person was doing to get rid of the problem, but no one asked that question.

The governors that signed the CRT laws can prepare for challenges to those laws because of the language used in the laws. Since the laws all address teaching about race, a term not yet defined, that would mean the words black and white should not be employed because they represent an example of discrimination. Black and white used as nouns are colors, but society conditioned them to represent fixed groups of people. The use of black and white as social identities are indefensible because they lack definitions. If the words are adjectives, in constructions such as black race and white race, then their use violates the CRT laws relative to the use of race. The word race does four things simultaneously; it unites, separates, discriminates, and controls whenever and wherever it is employed as a social identity.

Danielle Sered suggested an assortment of important and necessary elements to consider when attempting to address a wrong using restorative justice. The individual implements these elements after determining that European supremacy is wrong as well as the refusal to accept its falseness. They are like the basic elements but not exactly the same. The elements all demand personal accountability and "acknowledging responsibility for one's actions, acknowledging the impact of one's action on others, expressing genuine remorse, taking actions to repair the harm to the degree possible, and no longer committing similar harm" (237).

The fear that European Americans feel about having the truth of European supremacy revealed is very real, but the chance of it happening anytime soon is not likely simply because society conditioned Americans to look at race and racism as the cause of the ethnic bigotry when it is not. The suggestions given by scholars like DeAngelo and Sered reveal that their process of acknowledgment begins with accepting race as valid, and it not being part of the myth. The fact that they refer to themselves as white women and not just women underscore the point. When the myth of European supremacy is debunked, then race and all its accompanying derivatives are also debunked and should not continue to be employed as part of the language involving social identities.

DiAngelo missed the point in addressing ethnic bigotry by retaining her white identity and thinking that it would initially transfer from negative to positive by simply using the ethnic identity which she discarded in favor of a white identity. She then rejects the idea of a positive white identity and added that "[w]hite identity is inherently racist; white people do not exist outside the system of white supremacy. This does not mean that we should stop identifying as white and start claiming only to be Italian or Irish. To do so is to deny the reality of racism in the here and now..."this denial would simply be a color-blind racism." Her solution then is to become "less white" because this would "require me to be more racially aware, to be better educated about racism, and to continually challenge racial certitude and arrogance" (DiAngelo 149-50). So, the pattern of cognitive dissonance continues for her since she retains her belief and acceptance of European supremacy and race.

When we say that we must debunk the myth of European supremacy at the very beginning, we simply mean that we must replace it with the truth and reality, not retain, and expand. If we retain any form of belief in the myth, we will distort reality, and not realize truth.

While Sered focused her study on mass incarceration she also had to include the part played by ethnic bigotry. Her process of facing reality does not require a need for European Americans to change their white identity. Instead, she believes that white people should tell the truth about their experiences, especially those involving mass incarceration. She sees reckoning as a process to a better America. She stated that "I believe America has advanced as far as we can toward equity without facing the truth about our history. We got every drop of change we could out of our current story, and that the next step requires telling some greater truths. We are due for a reckoning" (253). One wonders how a reckoning can take place if the myth of European supremacy and race are still current. Also, how does one determine equity in a society governed from the beginning by standards that support ethnic bigotry?

What is apparent in the works of both DiAngelo and Sered is that they do not want to give up the power and control based on their whiteness. Regardless of the approaches offered to address the social problems involving race, they do not want to lose control of their freedom and whiteness.

Americans and Western culture are conditioned to view and accept ethnic bigotry as a part of the reality of life. In addition, the Europeans and European Americans shared a vision of both liberty and slavery. However, according to Tyler Stovall, "a vision of society in which this liberty was unequally distributed and deeply racialized. The result was freedom for those at the top of the racial hierarchy, supported by and premised upon the unfreedom of those at the bottom." He maintained that a constant duel between those two opposite realities "have been and continue to be counterparts in the making of modern history. To be free, Stovall notes, has long meant to be white, and to be white has conversely long meant to be free" (*White Freedom* 15). Because of this attachment to whiteness, it must be the first thing to remove from one's identity if debunking the myth of European supremacy.

The fear of losing power became a major concern when Barack Obama was elected president. Prior to that time the supporters of European supremacy saw no need to safeguard their myth because no threat challenged their power and control. However, Obama's election turned on the lights for those wanting to maintain the status quo. Obama's election was a shock to none other than the head of the senate, Mitch O'Connell who in a statement indicated that his primary objective was not to the country, but to make certain that Obama would not be reelected. The fear was exacerbated when Obama was elected to a second term. The far-right and other conservatives redoubled their activities in a variety of activities to not only discredit Obama, but also to underscore their power and control of the country.

When Donald Trump was elected president, he brought with him an attitude and behavior that projected European supremacy. His attitude and behavior emboldened others to exhibit their fear of losing their power and a sense of tribalism focused on protecting their whiteness. From the very beginning of American society, the Anglo-Saxons, the ruling class "took special pains to be sure that the people they ruled were propagandized in the moral and legal ethos of white-supremacism." They created laws to make them feel like they were special, like the ruling class in Europe. Theodore Allen commented that "[t]hus was the 'white race' invented as the social control formation whose distinguishing characteristic was not the participation of the slaveholding class, or even of other elements of the propertied classes" (*Invention* 251). Whether Trump was familiar with this aspect of history, he did understand the strength of working-class European Americans to hold the line on whiteness.

Long before Trump, the glue that held together the myth of European supremacy was the control exerted by the ruling class. Since they saw themselves as special and different from other people of color, they would support the wishes of the ruling class even at their own disadvantage. Allen referred to how the working-class people's desire to identify as white served as a safety valve for the ruling class to maintain control. The protection may be in danger in America and the Western world because of the changing demographics that is raising the fear level of the European supremacists. Isabel Wilkerson explained the changes taking place with respect to whiteness: "As it stands, the United States is facing a crisis of identity unlike any before. The country is headed toward an inversion of its demographics, with its powerful majority expected to be outnumbered by people not of European descent within two decades" (*Caste* 381).

We can witness evidence of the changing demographic of American life by simply looking at the images projected by social media. Prior to Obama's election, the images of people of different ethnicities were seldom; today, they have become almost common. Unfortunately, these new images bring fear to the surface for the European supremacists.

The fear comes from the American concept of majority rule. Wilkerson noted that "[w]hite dominance has already been assured by the inherited advantages of the dominant cast in almost every sphere of life, and in the securing of dominant interests in most aspects of governing—from gerrymandered congressional districts to voter suppression....the rightward direction of the judicial branch to the Electoral College, which favors the dominant caste [ruling class], whatever the numbers" (381-382). The fear of losing power is nonetheless a constant concern and the introduction of new laws addressing what and how to teach American history is a clear sign of it.

Control has always been key to America's power over people, places, and things as Wilkerson explained in referring to the caste system in America "Casteism is the investment in keeping the hierarchy as it is in order to maintain your own ranking, advantage, privilege, or to elevate yourself above others or keep others beneath you" (70). According to Michelle Alexander, "[p]ublic discussions about racial caste in America are relatively rare. We avoid talking about caste in our society because we are ashamed of our racial history. We also avoid talking about race" (*The New Jim Crow* 13). Any talk about history or caste must be avoided because it would obviously have to shed light on the truth of European supremacy.

However, another form of control in America is "the criminal justice system," but is nothing like justice for African Americans. The heart of this system of control is *mass incarceration* which Alexander renamed "The New Jim Crow." So, how does mass incarceration affect control in society? Alexander explained that "mass incarceration refers not only to the criminal justice system but also to the larger web of laws, rules, policies, and customs that control those labeled criminals both in and out of prison...Once released, former prisoners enter a hidden underworld of legalized discrimination and permanent social exclusion. They are members of America's new undercaste" (13). Fortunately, scholars like Wilkerson and Alexander have exposed these devastating systems to America and the world and by doing so have given rise to individuals and organizations wanting to change, if not replace these controlling systems. With an increase in grassroots organizations across America creating positive change, there has been a growing fear by European supremacists over a loss of control. These organizations are fighting for criminal justice reform, advocating for the restoration of voting rights, pushing to end pretrial incarceration, dismantling the school-to-prison pipeline, improving conditions in jails, and more. The success of these groups thrives on the fact that many of them include not only not only people of color but also Americans of all ethnicities including a variety of European Americans.

Extensive advocacy groups for criminal justice reform and many other groups like those listed on the Daily Kos like Chicago Community Bond Fund (Chicago, IL); EXPO (Ex-Incarcerated People Organizing) (Milwaukee, WI); Voice of the Experienced (New Orleans, LA); Youth Justice Coalition (Los Angeles, CA); The Texas Civil Rights Project (Austin, TX); Families for Justice as Healing (Roxbury, MA); Partnership for Safety and Justice (Portland, OR) Oklahoma Coalition Against People Abuse (Oklahoma City, OK) (Ashton Lattimore, Daily Kos, 12/17/2019) An extensive list prison reform groups can be located at this location: advocacy groups for criminal justice reform/bing.com

With advances in technology, changes in demographics, and the resurgence of interest in social change through political means, American society is changing rapidly, causing the myth of European supremacy to gradually lose its hold. Time is running out on the power the myth controls.

CHAPTER 7
DEBUNKING THE EUROPEAN SUPREMACY
MYTH

History tells us that the germ of the first supremacy myth began when Geoffrey of Monmouth authored a book called *History of the Kings of Britain*, in which he embellished the legend of King Arthur and laid the groundwork for its survival. The English and the Normans realized that they could expand history and manipulated history to serve a variety of purposes, especially politically. Because Geoffrey had ties to both groups, the people during the Middle Ages accepted the myth's origins "but the advent of the Renaissance and the Reformation brought its credibility under attack. It had its defenders in the seventeenth century, but with the confirmation of the Glorious Revolution its political vitality was spent" (McDougall 1-2). So, for a while, at least, the original myth was debunked.

The second myth focused on the Anglo-Saxons and was based on hereditary ties to Germany and embraced various elements that were neither factual nor verifiable. They were, however, well-developed concepts that appeared logical but really had no real bases. The primary features led to the Anglo-Saxon myth of superiority where they believed they inherited their superiority from the Germans because of their unmixed purity, superb character, and their ability to civilize people with whom they came into contact; that their origin and history began with Hengist and Horsa in 449 at Ebbsfleet; that they inherited from their Germanic ancestors the ability to invent institution of politics and religion that contributed to man's freedom; that because of their Germanic inheritance they were better than any other people could "assume leadership of the world community" (2). As with all myths, the value is untenable because they are based on conjecture.

We know that the heart of European supremacy is the invented term race, and we know that the term was to try and validate the myth. We also know that race has no fixed definition or relevance to biological science. While the term is employed as though it has validity, we know through history and science that it is bogus. Nonetheless, the myth survives and the reason for its survival has nothing to do with race. "the power of myths and their related ideologies lies not in their objective truth but in their being perceived as true" (3). We are now at a point where we can move past the time-consuming tactic of fighting against race and racism and go directly to the myth and expose its baseless and irrational concept. We know that the only way to debunk a myth is to expose it to the truth and historical facts. So why have some Americans been fighting racism for over two hundred years when it is not the problem? Race and racism are distractions from the problem of belief in the myth. The way to rid society of ethnic bigotry is to get rid of the language of race. The problems caused by race and racism are all actions used to exhibit the power and control that the European supremacy myth possesses. No problems attributed to race can ever be resolved by using the language of race. So, how does one get rid of race? The short answer is by examining its history and exposing its truth as pseudo-science. For individuals seeking to debunk the myth of European supremacy history is important relative to how they view themselves.

A simple example is one regarding a glass containing fifty percent water and fifty percent air. The question of whether the glass is half full or half empty is employed to determine the mindset of the person asked the question. Depending on the person's answer, the response is supposed to determine if the person is an optimist or pessimist. However, the answer given has no correct answer because it reflects the person's personal way of thinking and not the level of the water in the glass. To accurately answer the question, we have to examine why the glass is either half full or half empty. Was the water put into the glass or taken out of it to that level? We do not know, so we cannot accurately answer the question unless or until we learn the history of the glass prior to viewing its contents. History is important.

History plays an important part relative to an individual's identity and that knowledge is necessary before any attempt to discover the facts and truths regarding identity. Without a knowledge of history, acquiring the truth might be an exercise in futility. For example, recently, I had the opportunity to speak at a Kwanzaa celebration. I had just finished explaining the difference between our ancestral or ethnic identity and our nationality when a mature woman of color raised her hand and announced that she was black, her parents were black, and that she was proud of being black and that she loved being black. She directed her statements to me. So, I asked if I could ask her a question. She agreed; so, I asked her if she meant that she was black as a color or black as a social identity. She seemed puzzled. I continued by offering additional remarks regarding color in America.

I explained that when someone identifies themselves as black or white that signals a lack and loss of personal historical information for both people. For the people identifying as black, they signal a lack of historical knowledge relative to their blackness. Regardless of how they view themselves today with blackness, historically the term applied to their ancestors as enslaved Africans to deprive them of all their history. The terms black and negro do not provide any information relative culture, religion, ethnicity, or geography; it identifies the person as an enslaved person with no sense of history. Society conditioned Americans to use their ethnic identity as their official or legal identity instead of their nationality. The ethnic identity is based on a person's biological parentage; the nationality is based on where the person claims citizenship. For example, if a person were born in Japan to Japanese parents, the ethnic identity would be Japanese. However, if that person moved to America and became an American citizen, the nationality would be American, but the ethnic identity would still be Japanese, in other words, Japanese American. We all have at least two identities, one ethnic, the other national.

When I finished my explanation, the woman that had professed her blackness nodded her head towards me as a signal of understanding. The others in the audience that had initially agreed with the woman were silent.

In an analogous situation five or so years ago, I had given a lecture to a group of European Americans in a small rural town and was discussing the role of European Americans in a certain context pertaining to the lecture. A mature, white-haired woman raised her hand and asked a question. She commented that I had used the term European American at various times and wanted to know what that meant. I told her that it was an identification used for people who identified as white. I asked her how she identified herself and she answered, white. I asked, how do you know that you are white? She hesitated for a moment, then replied that her parents told her as a child that she was white. I asked did she mean her skin complexion was what defined her as white, and she answered, yes. Then she asked me why do you refer to me as European American.

I offered an explanation using American history relative to immigration during the early 1900s when the Johnson-Reed Act was passed. The explanation focused on people from eastern and southern Europe that immigrated to America, people not considered white by the Anglo- Saxons upon arrival to America. They were identified by their ethnic identity and nationality. For example, they were identified as Irish, Italian, Jew, and other ethnic identities, however, once they were in America, they quickly realized that the most valuable identity they could have is white. So, as quickly as they could, they abandoned their ethnic and national identity and assumed an identity of whiteness. Eventually, these immigrants were known as the lesser whites called Caucasian.

I explained why certain people abandoned their ethnic and national identity and chose white as their identity because white proved to be more valued than just being American. The term European American is employed to denote an ancestral and national identity where no specific ancestral identity is employed; the same goes for African American, if there is no direct African identity used. She thanked me for the brief history lesson.

The reason for these examples focusing on the importance of history is the fact that the first order of business is for individuals to acknowledge how they define and view themselves. What we witness today with many scholars and writers is an acceptance of race as legitimate. We can acknowledge the system of American bigotry, but not debunk the myth of European supremacy because we legitimize the language of race. To get a clear and factual picture of European supremacy, history must be the starting point.

English history tells us how the myth of Anglo-Saxon superiority began and how the exploitation of history and science supported the myth. History also shows us that the invented word race was to represent and replace the concept of a subspecies of Homo sapiens that does not exist. Therefore, history tells us that both the myth and race are not factual or true. If we want to debunk the myth of European supremacy, we must look at history that tells us the concept of a white and black race is false and has no factual evidence to support the claim. All the actions and behaviors relative to the myth of European supremacy and race are based on lies. Therefore, any belief in the myth or acknowledgment of it as valid must end.

In addition to finding the myth unacceptable, further acknowledgment that everything done underscoring the myth's power and control must be understood and seen as wrong. The list of unacceptable information includes, but is not limited to, the invention of race, the colonization of countries considered non-European and non-Christian, instituting systems of slavery, and using skin complexion as a determinant of race. By recognizing these elements of European supremacy as wrong and unacceptable, any further adherence to them should be discontinued. For most European Americans, the most challenging element to debunk and discard is race by color. Americans have been so conditioned to viewing themselves through the prism of color that seeing themselves as just a member of *the species* would be life changing. If the myth of European supremacy is to be debunked, then the people involved in the experience will, in fact, experience a change in how they view themselves and others.

Since the use of color cannot be the determining factor in viewing everyone as belonging to the same species, an acceptance of diversity in all its manifestations must take place. The acceptance must not be a form of color blindness, but an acceptance of all colors, cultures, religions, languages, and people as part of one human family. The term race should no longer be employed to denote an ethnic difference, but the use of the words ethnic or ethnicity. Neither of those terms carry with them a biological component, so any discrimination relative to ethnicity cannot be based on anything fabricated. Debunking the myth of European supremacy should serve to free European American from all the pretenses and defenses used to hide the truth. When race is no longer a part of the language neither will be black and white because they are the adjectives that precede the noun race. The correct term to identify members of the human family is species. The confusion created by pseudo-science regarding Homo sapiens and any reference to a separate human race is incorrect and inaccurate. No such thing exists.

Debunking the myth of European supremacy must be an individual undertaking because of the transformation that will take place—going from someone whose identity depends on skin complexion to someone that embraces all humanity as family is extremely difficult. In addition, realizing the complicity that comes with the former identity that aligned itself with injustices and ethnic bigotry across the social spectrum can be very disturbing but can also help in developing a sense of reckoning. Nonetheless, while a group cannot undertake the experience, an individual can serve to educate groups as to the need for seeing reality. So, how does one begin the transition process? The key is the language, that is, the avoidance and use of any words or phrases that denote race in any context.

For example, instead of using the word race, use instead ethnicity; instead of racism, use ethnic bigotry; instead of racial, use cultural or ethnic group; instead of saying black, use person of color, or their ethnic identity; instead of saying white, use European American or their ethnic identity. In cases where an ethnic identity is not necessary, simply use the nationality, like American.

So, what kind of effect will the avoidance of race language have on society? The article "The Rising of White America" by Michele Norris serves as an example of how the language is employed, Norris describes the fear experienced by certain European Americans. Norris describes the "[d]emographic changes rippling across the country as fueling fears among some, who see their culture and standing threatened." She brings the concept of race by color into the discussion by offering examples that underscore the myth.

"For decades, examining race in America meant focusing on the advancement and struggles of people of color. Under this framework, being white was simply the default. Every other race of ethnic group was 'other-ized,' and matters of race were the problem and province of people of color." Norris noted that the election of Barack Obama followed by the election of Donald Trump brought to the surface what it meant to be white. As part of her research, she stated that "I created the Race Card Project when the word 'post-racial was in vogue, but I knew America was anything but." She indicated that although Americans do not like or want to talk about race, her Race Card Project allowed people to talk "honestly about privilege, guilt, rage, myopia, displacement, allegiance, power, romance or simply the world as seen through a white gaze." The participants in the project, to her surprise, were not minorities.

The comments and sentiments of one participant, Brain Glover, seemed to express the views of various European Americans. "Whiteness as we know it depends on not being a minority...In the 20th century, the white man was the best deal that anybody ever had in the history of the planet. I mean, in America you could feel like you were the center of everything" (Brian Glover, professor of 18th century British Literature, East Carolina University, Greenville, North Carolina). Glover was born in 1970 to a family "of mixed European origin—Jewish, Irish, Greek, German, Slovene, people once not seen as fully white by the gatekeepers of social class. But over time they moved into the mainstream." He underscored what that move meant to him, "I definitely felt like I was white American, which I understood to mean just plain American."

He continued to explain that families like his slowly began to displace the Anglo-Saxons that have controlled society and the government for over two centuries. Now, with the changing demographics, he admits that things have changed: "'White' is no longer the default setting for 'America.' And though this process is inevitable—it's just a matter of numbers and demographics...The country is changing in ways that aren't good for me, and I've got no choice but to adapt." Glover's comments indicate that reality can be a bitter pill to swallow especially when one experiences the changes personally: going from majority to minority. Norris expressed his fears by saying "[t]he founding Fathers built white dominance into the fabric and laws of the nation, and a country that proclaims to love freedom and liberty is still struggling with its roots in the original sin of slavery." The truth and facts must be employed to replace and reject the belief in the myth of European dominance whenever and wherever it occurs.

Changes are at the heart of technology in America and the world; changes that affect every aspect of our lives. Today, we can activate and control everything in our homes, appliances, and our vehicles simply by using our voice. Our superhero of old, Superman, would be hard-pressed to find a telephone booth to change into his costume as well as grandpa trying to find the controls on the television set. The recent pandemic has shown us just how dependent we are on each other. It takes a community to put food on our tables and uphold justice, technology has made our community smaller. Technology impacts our lives in housing, education, income, job, health care, law, and criminal justice. The fact that technology has made our lives more transparent gives us hope that in time we can remove the injustices present in the criminal justice system and the myth of European supremacy debunked.

Technology has been used to capture wrongdoings and open people's eyes to the truth. Recently, for example, three European American men were sentenced to life in prison for the murder of a young African American man, Ahmaud Arbery. This murder and trial occurred in the South. Had it not been for the video produced at the trial that recorded the entire incident, these men would not have, no doubt, received any charges for any offense.

After the election of Barack Obama as President of the United States, a focus on politics seemed to take center stage in the lives of people of color. People of color filled the job of mayor in some of America's large cities as well as other elected positions in city, state, and the national government. People of color came to the realization that if positive changes were to come, they must come through the actions of the people wanting and needing the changes. To that end, segments of people of color, especially women became politically active in a plethora of ways. Women began developing civic and political groups that fight for the improvements they want to see accomplished.

An article by John Nichols called "16 Reasons to be Hopeful in 2022" featured a group of sixteen people of color and their involvement in addressing the changes they want to see enacted. The article's essence, stated by one of the featured individuals, Carol Anderson, was that "American democracy's most dangerous adversary is white supremacy… Throughout this nation's history, white supremacy has undermined, twisted and attacked the viability of the United States….What makes white supremacy so lethal, however, is not just its presence but also the refusal to hold its adherents fully accountable for the damage they have done and continue to do to the nation. The insurrection on 6 January and the weak response are only the latest example" (*The Nation*). In effect, the fear of losing power and control will increase by the efforts of people of color and their allies seeking positive changes in our society.

We cannot control many of the events that occur throughout time. We recognize that many of the things committed and hidden throughout our history are only now coming to light because time has released them. For too many years people have been trying to find ways to eliminate race and racism in America with no success. The lack of success comes from trying to eliminate a concept that does not lend itself to anything logical or practical. What has been associated with race and racism did not derive from race or racism, but the belief in a myth that viewed a group of human beings as superior to all other human beings. Since all human beings belong to the same species, the concept is illogical, irrational, and false. So, why believe it and promote it as though it is valid? Because the power and control it gave to the ruling group over other people. The myth of European supremacy cannot be debunked by individuals, but by the passage of time and by changes in demographic, technological, and political systems throughout our society.

Anthropologists and others have predicted the browning of America in two or less decades. Time will pass whether we want it to or not and change will become more apparent since it has always been in the process of bringing to the surface things previously hidden. For too long ethnic bigotry, and European supremacy has held America back from achieving great and beneficial things. Fortunately, changes are coming, although with understandable difficulty, but coming just the same, and for those who understand the changes it will be a welcomed sight. Those who are unable to let go of the past and continue to embrace the injustices will have to adjust sooner or later. Time will not stop for anyone, so why not use it for good.

AFTERWORD

The reference in the Bible from John 8:31-32, about truth setting someone free is not a far-gone conclusion. The key to being set free is believing in the truth and acting on it. When the truth is known but ignored, freedom is not possible. In America, the truth regarding the myth of European supremacy is a guarded public secret that everyone knows but conveniently ignores. Belief in the myth is the power that runs society and controls the people. So, if the truth of the myth is not threatened, the proponents and protectors of it feel secure. Although we sometimes find it hard to believe, ethnic bigotry began with the building of American society and has remained a well-woven thread in the fabric of the American experience.

Protecting and promoting the myth of European supremacy's truth from being revealed and acknowledged has always been the fear of its protectors and promoters. Following the occasions in history where civil rights entered the fight for justice and fairness, we find fierce defense offered to prevent it from moving forward. Without question, the fear of exposure was present during the early years of the nation, but because of the power and control in the hands of European American, Anglo-Saxon males, they could quickly and easily quash any threats.

Each occurrence initiated by people of color in America to gain basic rights and privileges faced rejections that maintained the status quo.

Even after the Civil War ended and freed the enslaved people, segments of American society took measures to deny basic rights and freedoms. The suggestion that the far right and proponents of European supremacy are recent developments is not based on facts.

In his recently published book, *Far-Right Vanguard, The Radical Roots of Modern Conservatism,* John S. Huntington wrote that "early successes of the civil rights movement—most notably *Brown v. Board of Education* also served to spur the far right, as white Southerners joined the Citizens' Council movement to challenge the Supreme Court and resist integration." His point is that efforts by proponents of European supremacy have not remained static but expanded today to include regular European American voters who agree with the philosophy exhibited by the far right.

The advances gained in civil rights since the 1950s increased the fear of the myth's exposure and subsequently, the loss of power and control. Proponents of the myth find ways to deflect or deny the possible gains through language or legal actions. Recent tactics to deny people of color their rights and liberties include mass incarceration, laws restricting voting privileges, and laws preventing the teaching of history dealing with race that shows America in a less-than-positive image. They employ a variety of these efforts and more to hide the truth of the myth of supremacy. However, regardless of the many tactics employed, the element of demographics places constant pressure on deniers of the truth. Once the truth comes to the light, the acknowledgment and acceptance of it will eliminate the need or desire to live in a fantasy world. When I was a young adolescent boy one of my favorite television shows was Superman. The most impressive thing about his character was his ability to fly. Like most young boys my age who watched the show, we had illusions and fantasies of flying. I believed if I concentrated hard enough and believed with all my heart that I could fly like Superman, I could. One afternoon, I dawned an old bath towel and secured it to the back of my shirt—it was my cape. I climbed atop our chicken house, about six feet above the ground, took a deep determined breath, ran three steps, and jumped into the air. Yes, I landed unhurt on the ground and was disappointed that I could not fly. That experience, however, taught me two important lessons: that human beings cannot fly and that regardless of how hard and strong we believe in a fantasy or myth, it can never come true today, many Americans are becoming aware of the fantasy world they have been living in and reality is rapidly coming to light. Although the experience is difficult and challenging, it is also liberating and stress- relieving. After over two-hundred years of playing make-believe, it is about time for America to face reality.

ABOUT THE AUTHOR

Paul R. Lehman earned his Ph.D. from Lehigh University in 1976. He is a university Professor Emeritus in the department of English, and a former Dean of the Graduate College at the University of Central Oklahoma in Edmond, Oklahoma. Dr.

Lehman's teaching experiences span a wide range of subjects from Ethnic American Literature, African American Literature, American Literature, Short Stories, American Fiction, and Chaucer.

He worked in the Oklahoma City area as a news journalist, news anchor and producer for the CBS affiliate KWTV during the late 1960s to 1970s. He was inducted into the Oklahoma Journalism Hall of Fame (Class of 2017) and the Oklahoma Higher Education Hall of Fame (Class of 2018). He presently lives in Edmond, Oklahoma and is active in community and ethnicity-related affairs. Contact information: **www.pmlehman@cox.net**

Some of Lehman's books include:

Demystifying Bigotry II: The Best of The American's Race Problem Blog (2015-2018)

Demystifying Bigotry: The Best of The America's Race Problem Blog (2009-2017)

The system of European American (white) Superiority and African American (black) Inferiority

Flannery O'Connor: Southern Racial Culture and African American Characters

America's Race Matters: Returning the Gits of Race and Color.

America's Race Problem: A Practical Guide to Understanding Race in America

The Development of a Black Psyche in the Works of John Oliver Killens

The Making of the Negro in Early American Literature

WORKS CITED

Abrams, Meyer Howard. *The Norton Anthology of English Literature: Fifth Edition*. W.W. Norton, 2006, p. 16.

Alexander, Michelle. *The New Jim Crow*. The New Press, 2012, pp. 13,70.

Allen, Theodore W. *The Invention of the White Race Volume 2: The Origins of Racial Oppression in Anglo-America*. Verso, 1997.

Baker, John R. *RACE*. Oxford University Press, 1974, pp. 24, 26, 504.

Banton, Michael. *Racial Theories*. Cambridge University Press, 1998.

Barzun, Jacques. *Race, a study in superstition*. New York, Harper & Row, 1965, pp. 35, 45.

Boyd, Rhea, et al. "Racism in Medicine." *Time*, 17 May 2021, p. 29.

Britannica, The Editors of Encyclopedia. "Treaty of Tordesillas". *Encyclopedia Britannica*, 21 Sep. 2022, www.britannica.com/event/Treaty-of-Tordesillas. Accessed 14 January 2022.

Broubalow, Justin. "The Johnson-Reed Act of May 24, 1924". We're History, 24 May 2018,

Cartwright, Samuel A. "A Report on Diseases and Peculiarities of the Negro Race" The New Orleans Medical and Surgical Journal, 1851, pp. 330-31.

Chua, Amy. *Battle Hymn of the Tiger Mother*, Penguin Group, 2011, pp. 52-53, 63.

Clayton, Aubrey. "How Eugenics Shaped Statistics." *Nautilus*, 28 Oct. 2021, nautil.us/how-eugenics-shaped-statistics.

"Cognitive dissonance." Merriam-Webster.com Dictionary, Merriam-Webster, Accessed 12 Jan. 2022.

Darwin, Charles. *The Origin of Species.* London, Harper Collins Publishers, 2011.

Darwin, Charles, R. <u>*De l'origine des espèces, ou des lois du*</u> (in French), Trans. Royer, Clémence-Auguste (1st French ed.), Paris: Guillaumin and Masson, 1862.

DiAngelo, Robin. *White Fragility: Why It's So Hard for White People to Talk About Racism.* Beacon Press, 2018, pp. 113. 149-50.

Dunbar, Paul Lawrence. "We Wear the Mask." New York, Dodd, Mead, and Company, 1913.

Fisher, Ronald A. "Positive Eugenics." *The Eugenics Review,* 1917.

Fitzgerald, Scott F. (Francis Scott), 1896-1940. The Great Gatsby. New York, Charles Scribner's sons, 1925.

Frantz Fanon's Theory of Cognitive Dissonance. www.cram.com Accessed 2022.

Galton, Francis. *Hereditary Genius.* MacMillan, 1892.

Galton, Francis. *Inquiries into Human Faculty and Its Development.* Macmillan, 1883, pp. 199-200.

Gannon, Megan. "Race Is a Social Construct, Scientists Argue: Racial categories are weak proxies for genetic diversity and need to be phased out." *Scientific American,* 5 Feb. 2016, https://www.scientificamerican.com/article/race-is-a-social

Geoffrey, of Monmouth, Bishop of St. Asaph, 1100?-1154. *The History of the Kings of Britain: an Edition and Translation of De Gestis Britonum (Historia Regum Britanniae).* Woodbridge, UK; Rochester, NY, Boydell Press, 2007.

Griffin, Paul R. *Seeds of Racism in the Soul of America.* Sourcebook, Inc. 2000, pp. 45-47.

Grissom, James *Follies of God,* Alfred A. Knopf, 2016

Harvey, Joy. *Almost a Man of Genius: Clemence Royer, Feminism and Nineteenth-Century Science.* Rutgers University Press, 1997.

Herrnstein, Richard J. and Charles A. Murray. *The Bell Curve: Intelligence and Class Structure in American Life.* New York, Free Press, 1994.

Hodson, Gordon. "Race as a Social Construct." *Psychology Today*, 5 Dec. 2016,

Holloway, Kali. "The Missing Story." *The Nation*, 10 Jan. 2022, www.thenation.com/content/front-burner/ Accessed 2022.

Jacobson, Matthew Frye. *Whiteness of a Different Color*. Harvard Press, 1998, pp. 97, 207.

Judge, Lora. "Eugenics", 2002, history.com.

Kenny, Michael G. "Racial Science in Social Context." The University of Chicago Press Journals, www.journals.uchicago.edu/doi/full/10.1086/428959 Accessed 2022.

Kohn, Marek. *The Race Gallery*. Random House UK, 1996.

Laden, Greg. "A Troubling Tome." *American Scientist*, Accessed 17 Jan. 2022.

Lehman, Paul. *The Making of the Negro in Early American Literature.* Pearson Custom Publishing, 2003, 121.

Linnaeus, Carl. *Systema Naturae.* Stechert-Hafner Service Agency, *1964.* Mather, Cotton. *The Negro Christianized: An Essay to Excite and Assist the Good Work, the Instruction of Negro-servants in Christianity [Four lines of Scripture texts].* Boston, B. Green, 1706. pp. 121, 123-124, 133. Mead, Margaret. *Coming of Age in Samoa: A Psychological Study of Primitive Youth for Western Civilization.* William Marrow and Co., 1928, pp. x-xi, 6-7.

McAfee, Sarah. "Race Is a Social Construct." *Center for Health Progress,* 24 Oct. 2017, https://centerforhealthprogress.org/blog/race-social-construct/

Morton, Samuel. *Crania Americana.* Philadelphia, J. Dobson, 1839. McAuley, James. "Europe's War on Woke." *The Nation*, 29 Nov. 2021. Mills, Charles. The Racial Contract. Cornell University Press, 1999, pp. 27, 35, 122, 125. Wall text from human skeleton exhibit. Museum of Osteology, Oklahoma.

Murray, Charles. "A Book Review: 'A Troublesome Inheritance' by Nicholas Wade, A Scientific Revolution is underway– upending one of our reigning orthodoxies." The Wallstreet Journal, 2 May 2014, Murphy, Francis Xavier. "Alexander VI". *Encyclopedia Britannica*, 1 Jan. 2023, www.britannica.com/biography/Alexander-VI.

Nash, Gary B. *The Great Fear: Race in the Mind of America*. Holt, Rinehart and Winston, Inc. 1970.

Nania, Rachel. "U.S. Life Expectancy Sees Biggest Drop Since WWII." *AARP*, 21 July 2021, www.aarp.org/health/conditions

Newitz, Annalee. "The 9 Most Influential Works of Scientific Racism, Ranked." *GIZMODO*, 13 May, 2014, gizmodo.com/the-9-most-influential-works-of-scientific-racismrank-1575543279.

Nichols, John. "16 Reasons to Be Hopeful in 2022." *The Nation*. 28 Dec. 2021, www.thenation.com/article/society/2022-honor-

Norris, Michele. "The Rising Anxiety of White America." National Geographic, April 2018, www.nationalgeographic.com/magazine/article/race-rising

Obama, Michelle. "Unity With A Purpose", *Time*, 15 Feb. 2021, pp. 75- 80.

"Pseudo-scientific racism and Social Darwinism", *South African History Online*, Accessed 11 Jan. 2022.

Rauschenbusch, Walter. *Christianity and the Social Crisis*. New York, Hodder & Stoughton, 1907.

Reich, David. *Who We Are and How We Got Here*. Pantheon, 2019, p. 61.

Roberts, Andrew. *The Last King of America: The Misunderstood Reign of George III*. Viking, 2021, p. 24.

Saini, Angela. "The Story of Human Difference," *National Geographic*, Oct. 2021, p. 16.

Sered, Danielle. *Until We Reckon: Violence, Mass Incarceration, and a Road to Repair*. The New Press, 2019, pp. 220-19, 237, 253.

St. John de Crèvecoeur, J. Hector and Warren Barton Blake. *Letters From an American Farmer*. London, New York, J.M. Dent & Sons, Ltd., 1912. Stoddard, Theodore Lothrop. New York, Charles Scribner's Sons, 1920, pp. 165, 308.

Strong, Josiah. *Our Country*. Bake & Tyle Co. for the American Home Missionary Society Edition, 1885. "Strong, Josiah." *Encyclopedia.com*. Accessed 17 Jan. 2022.

Strong, *Josiah. The New Era or, The Coming of the Kingdom*. New York, Baker & Taylor, 1893, pp. 30-31, 345, 347. "Biography of Josiah Strong." *Swift Papers*. www.swiftpapers.com/biographies/Josiah-Strong-31363 Accessed 17 Jan. 2022.

Stovall, Tyler. *White Freedom, The Racial History of an Idea*. Princeton University Press, 2021, p. 15.

The University of Cambridge. *The Darwin Correspondence Project*. www.darwinproject.ac.uk/cl-mence-auguste-royer. Accessed 15 Jan. 20222.

VEL. "The Bell Curve: A Book Much Read About, But Rarely Actually Read." *The Contemporary Heretic*, 2021, thecontemporaryheretic.com/2021/07/07/the-bell-curve-a-bookmuch-   read-about-but-rarely-actually-read/comment-page-1. Accessed 15 Jan. 2022.

Wade, Nicholas. *A Troublesome Inheritance: Genes, Race and Human History*. Penguin Press, 2014, pp. 68-69.

"When History Meets Race Pseudo-Science." Pharos, 30 Oct. 2020, https://pharos.vassarspaces.net/2020

Wilkerson, Isabel. *Caste: The Origins of Our Discontent*. Random House, 2020, pp. 70, 381-382.

Williams, Patricia J. "How NOT to Talk About Race." *The Nation*. 18 Oct. 2021,

Willoughby, Christopher D. "His Native, Hot Country" 1: Racial Science and Environment in Antebellum American Medical Thought." Journal of the History of Medicine and Allied Sciences, 2017, pp. 330-31.